GOOD-BYE
TO ALL THAT

Written,
Art Directed
and Produced by
Harris Lewine
Designed by
Alan Peckolick

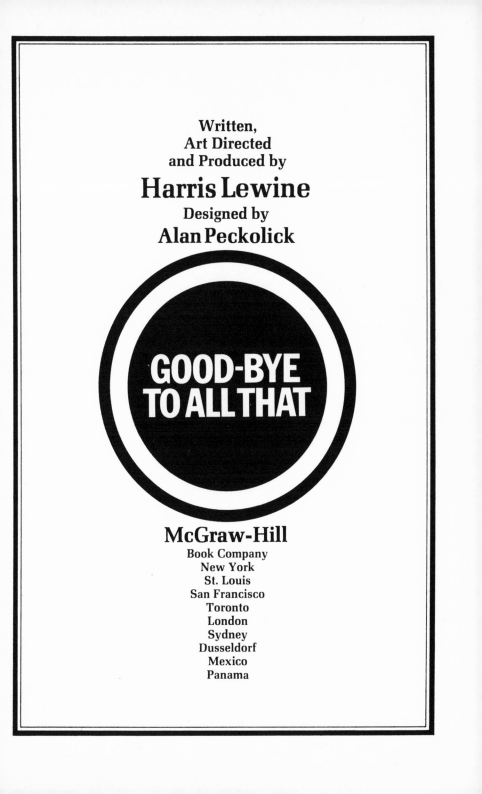

GOOD-BYE
TO ALL THAT

McGraw-Hill
Book Company
New York
St. Louis
San Francisco
Toronto
London
Sydney
Dusseldorf
Mexico
Panama

For thy sake, tobacco, I would do anything but die.
—Charles Lamb,
A FAREWELL TO TOBACCO, 1830

FREUD ON.

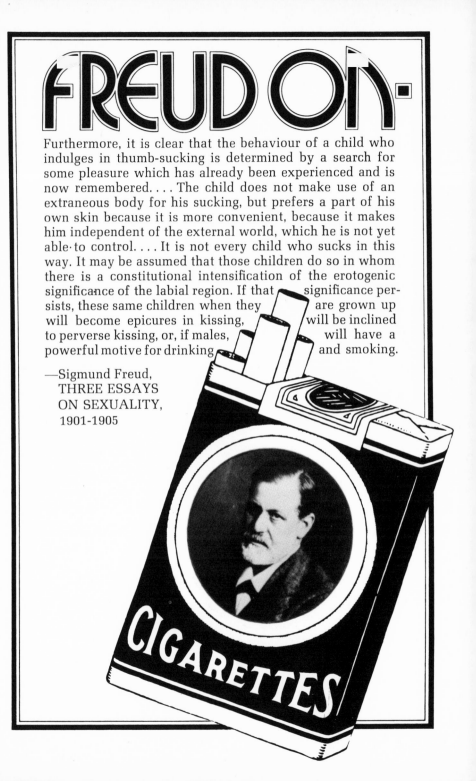

Furthermore, it is clear that the behaviour of a child who indulges in thumb-sucking is determined by a search for some pleasure which has already been experienced and is now remembered. . . . The child does not make use of an extraneous body for his sucking, but prefers a part of his own skin because it is more convenient, because it makes him independent of the external world, which he is not yet able·to control. . . . It is not every child who sucks in this way. It may be assumed that those children do so in whom there is a constitutional intensification of the erotogenic significance of the labial region. If that significance persists, these same children when they are grown up will become epicures in kissing, will be inclined to perverse kissing, or, if males, will have a powerful motive for drinking and smoking.

—Sigmund Freud,
  THREE ESSAYS
  ON SEXUALITY,
  1901-1905

CIGARETTES

Basil, I can't allow you to smoke cigars. You must have a cigarette. A cigarette is the perfect type of a perfect pleasure. It is exquisite, and it leaves one unsatisfied. What more can one want?

—Oscar Wilde,
THE PICTURE OF DORIAN GRAY, 1890

Oscar Wilde and Sherlock Holmes were born in 1854! That same year at Balaclava, in the Crimea, the British had "cigarettes to the right of them, cigarettes to the left of them, cigarettes in front of them"—hand-rolled gifts from their Turkish, French and Italian allies. And "half a league, half a league, half a league onward"... Russian cigarettes! "Forward the Light Brigade!" British cavalry officers became enamoured of this new aromatic "smoke," redolent of the mysterious East, which could stand up (unlike their breakable clay pipes) to the rigors of the Empire's far-flung campaigns. Back in London, the new paper cigarettes, all "hand-rolled," became *beau* fashion in salons and men's clubs.

Cigarettes of sorts date back to the Aztecs, the Mayas and the Pueblo Indians of New Mexico. They smoked hollow reeds filled with tobacco, crude cigarettes with maize wrappers and cigarettes made with cane shafts which were really "self-burning" pipes. The antecedent of the paper cigarette came from Seville, the cigar manufacturing capital of the seventeenth and eighteenth centuries. Cigar "butts" and tobacco scraps were wrapped in throwaway paper and given the name *papalete* or *cigarrillo*. These "beggar's smokes" flourished among the poor of southern Spain and in time filtered through to Portugal, Italy, Southern Russia and the Orient via Spain's far-reaching trading activities. But it took an improvising Egyptian cannoneer at the siege of the Turkish city of Acre in 1832 to roll the first paper cigarette! For improving his rate of fire by rolling his powder in paper tubes, or "pistils," his gun crew had been rewarded with a gift of pipe tobacco. Their only clay pipe destroyed by Turkish shot, the Egyptian soldiers proceeded to roll the pipe tobacco in the powder paper. The invention caught on with both Egyptians and Turks and by 1843 *dernier cri* France had made cigarette

7/24/70. My smoking "specs" read like a line of bold face in "Who's Who in Baseball": 459,900 cigarettes; 22,995 packs; $11,497.50; 28 years in the league; S.A.—60 cigarettes a day; smoked for Luckies, Chesterfield and Gauloises; sent down a total of 7 years for not smoking; candidate for enshrinement at Richmond, Raleigh or Durham. But I'm placing myself on the voluntary inactive list as of tomorrow morn-

manufacture a government monopoly with the birth of *Régie Française Des Tabacs*. The word "cigarette" is of French origin, and from the beginning of French manufacture cigarette girls poured tobacco into preformed paper tubes or cylinders, as opposed to the 1866 factory hand-rolled "tailor-mades" of the British and Americans.

The first British cigarette factory was opened in 1856 by Robert Gloag, a veteran of the Crimea, who used a smoke-cured form of Turkish tobacco called Latakia for his brand, *Sweet Threes*. In the late 1850s a veteran London tobacconist, Philip Morris, went into "hand-made" to order production of Turkish cigarettes, importing experienced Russian and Polish rollers from the tobacco factories of St. Petersburg. The next decade saw an increasing number of tobacconists in Old Bond Street hand-rolling on order for the officers and dandies.

Back in the States, Americans were still in the throes and with the spittoons of cigars and quid, or "chaw." The Mexican war of 1848 popularized cigars when troops came back smoking cigarros and cigarrillos, and soon New York and Philadelphia became manufacturing centers of "long nines," "short sixes" and "supers" of straight Havana or home-grown Connecticut Valley leaf with Havana filler. The push to the West saw foot-long "stogies" jutting from drivers' faces, smokes named after their Conestoga wagons.

Much earlier, in the 1820s, John Quincy Adams had made the brown rolled imported Havanas (Sevillas) proper in Boston and popular with the rising New England Industrialists, but it took the Civil War, and Ulysses S. Grant in particular, to make the nation cigar-conscious. With the blockade of New Orleans, the War between the States often became an exchange between a Northern "segar" and Southern "chaw."

ing! Why????? Because, unlike Italo Svevo's "Zeno," I am not dedi-cated to that Last Cigarette or the neurotic fuss made over stopping smoking, but rather side with Ian Fleming's "first delicious smoke!" I'll enlist tomorrow, whether for weeks or years, and save my savor-ing for that eventual return to the "pale" and the "hack." Meanwhile —Cold Turkey requires a concentration on Lifesavers, Hacks cough

U.S. cigarette manufacturing dates from the Civil War period in New York City, when Greek and Turkish tobacco shops hand-rolled mostly all-Turkish smokes for the "carriage trade." One such tobacconist/manufacturer—O. Bedrossian—specified on his trade card all the tobaccos then prevalent: Turkish, Ha-vana, Perique, Cavendish, Cut Navy, Persian, Natural Leaf (Vir-ginia or Bright), Latakia and St. James. And an imposing variety of cigarette sizes and shapes, some with cork tips and mouth-pieces, and all with continental or "tony" names: *Neapolitan, Militaires, Polonaises, Union Club, Comme Il Faut, Non Plus Ultra, Sultana, Entre Actos, Havana Imperiales, Turkish Elé-gantes, Jockey Club, Ladies, No Name 24s, Moscows, Operas, St. Petersburg, Petit Canons, No Name 10s* and *Uncle Sam.* A lexicon of French, English and Russian high life! Total U.S. cigarette consumption had reached somewhere between 18 and 20 million units in 1865, the first year that records were kept— roughly equal to the cigar's "novelty era" sales after the War of 1812.

The 1870s saw six manufacturing firms controlling seventy-five per cent of an expanding cigarette market, utilizing experi-enced immigrant rollers. Kimball of Rochester had: *Vanity Fair, Fragrant Vanity Fair, Cloth of Gold, Three Kings, Turkish Ori-entals* and *Old Gold.* Allen & Ginter of Richmond, a late starter in 1875, abandoned an early Havana brand and concentrated on straight Bright or Virginia with *Richmond Gem, Richmond Straight Cut No. 1, Our Little Beauties, Bon Tons, Napoleons* and *Opera Puffs.* In 1883 they opened a London factory for their popular Virginia brands and gained continental acceptance with distribution in western Europe and as far as Australia. Kinney of New York had: Kinney's *Straight Cut, Full Dress, Halves, Caporals, Sportsman's Caporal* and Kinney's *Sweet Caporal.*

drops, Adams Blackjack and a range of Magic Marker-colored sour-
balls. They become intermission energy to a distant time, say about
3 weeks, when one begins to regain a sense of taste and smell. But that
first week! Nothing tastes! Metabolism sinks! And like in some
athlete's-foot commercial we await a Billie Burke fairy-Godmother
enzyme to stir up and put to flight all those complacent, not-yet-tired-

Goodwin, also of New York, had more "down home" trade
names: *Canvas Back, Old Judge* and *Welcome.* Marburg and
Felgner, both of Baltimore, catered to the metropolitan markets,
Marburg with: *Estrella, High Life* and *Golden Age;* Felgner with:
Sublime, Principal and *Herbe de la Reine.*

By 1880, cigarettes were *beginning* to play "catch-up" with
the cigar industry. The four leading firms, doing eighty per cent
of the nation's business, totaled about 532,718,000 cigarettes.
Unit sales of cigars were about 2,400,000,000; however the leaf
poundage per unit was much greater in the cigar. Four years
earlier, an astute Currier and Ives print—"A Grand Centennial
Smoke"—had pictured Uncle Sam with an outsized "stogie"
and an unhappy (she detested smoking) Queen Victoria puffing
on a cigarette.

Oscar Wilde and Sherlock Holmes, charter members of The
First Cigarette Generation, came of smoking age in the still per-
missive London of the 1870s. France had received a temporary
setback at Sedan, but things French—art, novels, dress, habits,
music, painting, food and their cigarettes—continued to flourish
and wouldn't be considered naughty or immoral in London until
a somber period of reaction set in with Wilde's imprisonment
in the Nineties.

The cigarette was at home in Paris; though something of a
social novelty, it never had to endure the Anglo-Saxon stigma
of effeminacy or the American racial slur. A nationalized industry in 1843, cigarette smoking knew no class barriers and was in
evidence from Saint-Cyr to the laundresses in Grenelle and as a
dignified prop in the painting of Manet, Renoir and Henri Rous-
seau. "Look, she's going to smoke!" drew no exclamations from
the Frenchman. *Cigarette,* the waif heroine of Ouida's (Louise
de la Ramée) novel *Under Two Flags,* "Rides like an Arab,

-from-roistering Nicotine-ies. While we're waiting, a little Americana music, professor!—say, "These Foolish Things." I was born a double Sagittarius (Moon in Virgo, Venus in Scorpio) in an upstate New York city of flowers and raised in a southern Westchester city of bedrooms. It is always Saturday morning when I recall my childhood in the Thirties. And it is always morning when I recall "his" cigar habit. My

Smokes like a Zouave." *Cigarette* was "*Enfant de L'armée, Femme de la Fume, Soldat de la France.*"

The cigarette specifically and tobacco in general waft through the Victorian twilight of *The Adventures of Sherlock Holmes* and accurately reflect the tobacco mores of London's privileged majority—those possessing an income and those able to work for one! The most familiar object associated with Holmes is the pipe. The tobacco in the foot of the Persian slipper, the cocaine and the morphine induce dreamlike, thoughtful states necessary to Holmes's problem solving: "It is quite a three-pipe problem, Watson, and I beg that you won't speak to me for fifty minutes." For the other side of Sherlock Holmes—the "let's be off, Watson" man of action—there is the silver cigarette case, stocked with *Alexandrians,* that the "citified" Holmes feels might come in handy in his role as the aristocrat above the power of money and the champion of the morality of feudal ethics. It is symbolic that the forlorn silver cigarette case is left behind covering a message that points the way to Holmes's death plunge with Professor Moriarty over the Reichenbach Falls. The cigarette is used directly in solving "The Adventure of the Golden Pince-Nez." Holmes chain-smokes cigarette after cigarette proffered by the bed-ridden Professor Coram, who is a cigarette connoisseur. Suspecting someone hidden in the room (a prodigious stack of luncheon plates), Holmes, while smoking and pacing, plants a ring of cigarette ash around a suspect bookcase. Holmes and Watson go out on the ruse of searching the grounds and return to find the ring of ashes broken and the murderess behind the bookcase.

Oscar Wilde's war cry, *The Picture of Dorian Gray,* ushered in and inflamed the Nineties. Wilde made war on Dr. Watson and all the Sentimental Tommies, stiff upper lips, pipes and

15

father came awake like an Alger hero, or as if he had read one of those Housman "up lad and away" poems before retiring. By 7:00 he was shaved, Saville-Row flanneled and spatted and already into his first after-breakfast Webster Golden Wedding or Seidenberg Fancy Tail cigar. Clouds of smoke and guffaw-grunts accompanied the previous night's doing's of Alley Oop and Oola in the land of Moo. At 7:00 in

walking sticks in sight. He was for cigarettes ("Basil, I can't allow you to smoke cigars"), long hair and the belief that artists should be free and above *all* responsibility. He reigned supreme for four years. Then Lord Alfred Douglas, the trial and Reading Gaol. Released in 1897, Wilde found that long hair was out, anything French was out, cigarettes were for boys, at best, and Kipling, Rider Haggard, the Boer War and manly smut were in.

Conan Doyle's brother-in-law, William Hornung, spoke for the new Edwardian image of manliness *and* the cigarette when his gentleman-thief A. J. Raffles, tiring of a decade of aristocratic thievery, lies with his wounded friend Bunny on the veldt above Pretoria, surrounded by Boers, and offers the last of his beloved *Sullivan* cigarettes: "Feel equal to a cigarette? It will buck you up, Bunny. No, that one in the silver paper, I've hoarded it for this. Here's a light; and so Bunny takes the *Sullivan!* All honor to the sporting rabbit!"

American cigarette manufacturing entered the decade of the Eighties with a two-fold problem: production and distribution. The "carriage trade" all-Turkish brands weren't affected since their high cost, low volume and "made-to-order" specifications could be handled by the two dozen, at most, experienced Greek, Turkish or Bulgar rollers on the tobacconist's premises. And their high price compensated: *Khedive, Sultana, Moscows* and *Monopole* cost from 50¢ to 75¢ for 20; *Turkish Elégantes* were $1.00 for 20; and *Huppmann Imperiales*—$1.20 for 20—even by today's prices a "specialty" item! But the packaging and cigarettes themselves were a thing of beauty. Gold and silver paper-lined boxes; blind and foil stamping of the marque on the paper; cigarettes tightly rolled in an unending variety of sizes, strengths and tapered shapes, with gold, cork, silver and Russian-style mouthpieces. The undercovers and back covers of the boxes

the morning my father had the world by his Seidenberg Fancy Tail.
On most mornings a ritual would occur which probably hastened my
cigarette habit. It became one of those childhood endurance contests
like the Czerny exercises and the metronome. Tall and Texas-thin, with
a Menjou waxed moustache and Gable ears, a profusion of "ain'ts"
and the flamboyant manners of a nineteenth-century riverboat gam-

covered with awards—"19 Grands Prix"; regal crests with "By
Special Warrant to H.R.H. Prince Charles of Bavaria, The King
of Spain, The King of Italy," etc. Well worth it to the New Yorker
of the 1880s "who had everything."

The Big Four manufacturers—Kinney and Goodwin, both of
New York, Kimball of Rochester, and Allen & Ginter of Richmond—were concerned with the man "who had very little" and
were trying to develop a common-man product to compete with
the hundreds of smoking-tobacco brands led by Blackwell's *Bull
Durham*, from which one could hand-roll three times as many
cigarettes for the same price. Nickel denominations were the
standard pricing multiples for the majority of the straight Bright
best-selling smokes: 5¢ for a box of 10, and 10¢ for a box of 20.

Large scale cigarette production was limited by the difficult,
time-consuming and expensive process of hand-rolling "tailor-
mades." The experienced rollers of the previous decade, the
Russians and Poles, were either unwilling to leave New York,
where they could work for the smaller and more intimate Turkish
tobacconists, or had found more lucrative employment in the
other rising trades. Girls were hired—being the cheapest labor
force—and were factory-trained with the shredded leaf, the
flattened drumstick straightener, and the touch of flour and
water (for sealer). A highly skilled cigarette girl working at top
speed could manage four cigarettes a minute! Speed and super-
vision (Allen & Ginter had 500 girls in 1883) were becoming
giant obstacles to production and to holding the retail price of
cigarettes to its nickel multiples.

An admitted failure at twenty-four years of age is a rarity!
But then he had failed with something old; he would not fail
with something new! James Buchanan Duke of W. Duke & Sons,
Durham, North Carolina, grew up watching his father, Washing-

bler, my father, by some ruse such as a "man-to-man" talk, would seat me near him and proceed carefully to unwrap the cellophane from his second cigar of the day. He would light up, meanwhile twisting the cellophane to an approximation of a Simon Legree or a waxed moustache effect. Then he'd blow smoke in the open end, twist and seal it and apply the whole smoking moustache in one tickling swipe back

ton Duke, and his brothers battle W. T. Blackwell's *Bull Durham* smoking tobacco. Heavily advertised *Bull Durham* made Durham, North Carolina, "the town renowned the world around." Its bronze bull on a black background drew scores of imitators: *Magic Durham, Jersey Bull Durham, Pride of Durham, Billy Boy Durham, Dream Durham, Nickel-Plated Durham* and *Dime Durham*—all with bronze-on-black labels and the bull emblazoned. W. Duke and Sons' two smoking tobaccos, *Pro Bono Publico* and *Duke of Durham,* had the same color labels but refused to carry the bull. Wearying of the uphill battle, young Duke decided to join them. But in a different way! He went into the cigarette business!

In 1881 James Buchanan "Buck" Duke imported a factory manager and 125 experienced rollers from New York and set up manufacturing *Duke of Durham* cigarettes. About the same time, James Bonsack of Virginia invented a cigarette-making machine said to reduce manufacturing costs from 80¢ to 30¢ per thousand units. Bonsack contacted the Big Four manufacturers, but they hesitated to lease, fearing that the cigarette public would resent the exchange of "hand-mades" for a machine product. Duke took a chance on the machines at 24¢ per thousand and after ironing out the bugs was able to produce 200 cigarettes a minute!

His manufacturing revolutionized, Duke turned to packaging, promotion and advertising. But first, believing that the urban market held the future of the cigarette, he moved his whole operation in 1884 to a factory loft on Rivington Street in New York City. In rapid succession, Duke invented the slide-and-shell box (still in use with foreign brands, notably *Gitanes* and *Players*), sent his sales chief to Europe and Africa to canvass markets, had domestic salesmen hit retailers and jobbers, popularized dormant sales promotion devices such as the premium coupon

*and forth across my upper lip! With his other hand he would apply,
ring-like to my finger, the cigar band! Now to a 7 year old who im-
agined himself to be Huck Finn and knew himself to be Tom Sawyer,
the only recourse was to go right out and "skin a knee." Most every
day that "Lewine boy" became that "Johnson and Johnson" boy. Boyhood continued on the insulated playing fields of Westchester—pre-*

and the celebrity picture, invested heavily in billboard and newspaper advertising (spending an unheard of $800,000 in 1889), and
added the brands *Cyclone, Cameo, Cross Cut, Pedro, Town Talk*
and *Pin Head.* The "down home" named *Pin Head* was proudly
inscribed, "These cigarettes are manufactured on the Bonsack
Cigarette Machine." By 1889 annual production was 2,413,349,-
000, and Duke had forty per cent of the market. The Big Four
split the remainder of the business and in 1890 joined W. Duke
and Sons, without a battle but with many a twinge about the
Bonsack machine, to form a new corporation, The American
Tobacco Company. Capitalization was $25 million, and James
Buchanan Duke was named President.

Duke's success owed much to his early insight about pounding
home the pre-sell and repeat-sell lure of premiums, celebrity
picture cards and package deals, which heretofore had been used
almost exclusively in the smoking-tobacco and plug markets.
As far back as 1860, P. Lorillard had reached a sales inducement
apogee when it placed $100 in bills in random packages of its
new, fine-cut smoking tobacco, *Century.* The craze for *Century*
and its prize was cut short by authorities as being too much like
a lottery. Cigarette Trade Cards, or celebrity picture cards, date
from about 1878, when one Edward Bok suggested to a manufacturer that the blank "cardboard stiffeners" in the "cigarette
sandwich" might have biographies on one side and pictures on
the other. The American News Company–distributed *Marquis
of Lorne* cigarettes were the first to have the new picture cards
in each pack. Soon Duke's own *Duke of Durham* had a postage
stamp series, and Allen & Ginter had a celebrated American
Indian Chief series. By the middle of the 1880s photo-engraved,
photo–hand colored or lithographed trade cards could be found
in almost all brands of cigarettes and covered every conceivable

tentious English Tudor mansions where we played soccer and Black Diamond in the paneled game rooms while live-in maids were told to save the "long ones" (partially smoked cigarettes) when they cleaned up after parties and chauffers shammied and redusted the never-driven Packard Super 8's, Franklins and Buick Centurys. Friends' mothers seemed to be always reclining with bon bons or headaches.

subject: actresses and athletes, Indian chiefs, banners, medals, state mottos, generals, fruits and flowers, geography, stamps, birds and beasts. Baseball players, boxers, actresses and colleges were numbered to induce "chain buying." Also in each pack were coupons, a certain number entitling gifts as varied as photo albums, a Harvard pennant, silk flags, miniature oriental rugs and, later, even silk stockings!

In his *The Books in My Life,* Henry Miller remembers cigarette trade cards: "That first burlesque show I shall never forget. (*Krausemeyer's Alley,* with Sliding Billy Watson). From the moment the curtain rose I was trembling with excitement. Until then I had never seen a woman undressed in public. I had seen pictures of women in tights from childhood, thanks to *Sweet Caporal* cigarettes, in every package of which there used to be a little playing card featuring one of the famous soubrettes of the day." Trading cards would reach a peak of popularity around the turn of the century, tapering off before World War I, disappearing after, and remaining as coupons with *Herbert Tareyton* till 1939, and with *Raleigh,* even today. The cigarette trade card changed products in the 1930s to become the Bubble Gum Card of Gum, Inc., Philadelphia, which featured "war cards" of the Spanish Civil War and Chinese-Japanese War, G-Man cards and the usual array of athletes. Trade cards persisted to the point of mania in England before World War II. Ardath Tobacco, Carreras, Rothman's, W. O. Wills, Gallaghers, Players and Churchman all had cards ranging from film, stage and radio stars to a "first-aid" series. Cards were traded, auctioned and sold just like stamps through *The Cigarette Card News,* a monthly founded in 1933 for cigarette card collectors. Even Hitler's Germany was well documented, the cigarette trade cards of *Salem* of Dresden spotlighting the Nazi elite.

Although American cigarette sales doubled to 5 billion smokes

20

And fathers were austere if working and austere if they weren't. Traffic and noise were at a minimum except for an occasional police-escorted Tommy Manville, his Rolls Royce Landau going or coming from one wife or another. But Boyhood Follies and Boyhood Dreams were Depression-Proof! The hours spent trying to walk pigeon-toed after the style of our great grammar school athlete. And Carl Hubbell,

in the Nineties, the cigarette would spend the decade battling racial, sexual and economic attacks. The all-Turkish cigarette was a "big city," New York City, phenomenon accounting for twenty-five per cent of the sales between 1895 and 1910. Its immigrant origin, foreign names and foreign vapors stirred a "yellow journalism" invective that approached James I of England's *Counterblaste to Tobacco:* ". . . what honour or policie can move us to imitate the barbarous and beastly manners of the wilde, godlesse, and slavish Indians, especially in so vile and stinking a custome?" The Turkish smokes in particular were under duress as un-American and effeminate, and through the efforts of Lucy Gaston, an anti-cigarette pioneer, they were banned in twelve states. The all-American plug, pipe tobacco and the cigar were in the clear, however, since their use ran the social gamut from Grover Cleveland in the White House to the chaw "whittlers" at the country store. "Smoke like a Turk" became a popular epithet!

The rising middle classes of overstuffed Victorian interiors, affected by the hundred-odd Horatio Alger novels full of "pluck, luck and Protestant ethic," thought that cigarettes, like the kid gloves of Alger's rich-boy villains, were signs of a sallow heart and depravity. And in Stephen Crane's Bowery tale of 1890, *Maggie: A Girl of the Streets,* a toff is described, far from "Rum Alley" and "Devil's Row" in the Bowery: "A tall young man, smoking a cigarette with a sublime air, strolled near the girl. He had on evening dress, a moustache, a chrysanthemum, and a look of *ennui,* all of which he kept carefully under his eye."

Mark Twain still had his pipe, Dreiser's Charles Drouet and George Hurstwood kept their fine cigars in *Sister Carrie,* and, in San Francisco, Frank Norris's *McTeague* held on to his huge porcelain pipe. But the twentieth century was around the corner, and the cigarette, like "Hurry Up" America, couldn't wait.

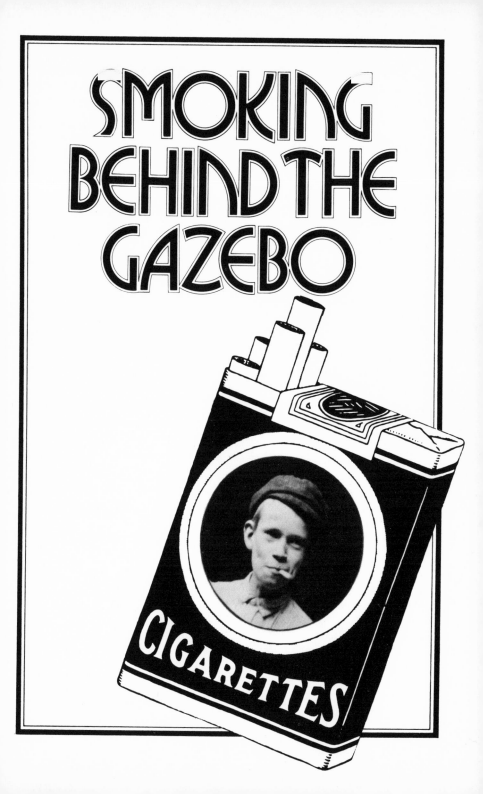

No boy or man can expect to succeed in this world to a high position and continue the use of cigarettes.
—Connie Mack, Mgr. Philadelphia Athletics,
SCIENTIFIC TEMPERANCE JOURNAL, 1913

prodigious cigar smoker sat in the White House (McKinley was said to be suffering heart trouble from the habit) while Messrs. Hearst and Pulitzer pulled off "their splendid little" Spanish-American War; the man in the street had his promised "Full Dinner Pail"; and millions of Americans cycled, picnicked, exercised, bathed and basked in an unprecedented prosperity. But cigarettes were still referred to as "paper cigars filled with skunk-cabbage," and photo-postcards pictured "strutting sissies" smoking.

Cigarette headway would be made *with* and *by* the younger generation—via speed: wheels, wings, the wireless and the train shrinking the continent; shorter work hours; "regiments" of shop boys; Bell Telephone "Hello Girls" saying, "Hello, Frisco, Hello"; the quick-lunch counter; the first subway (the Tremont Line—Boston, 1897); elevators in department stores and "quick" anticipating "everywhere." Stolid and conservative were on the way out! Sleek and rambunctious were coming in!

Earlier there had been a Cigarette Triumph: speed and "dash" saw "Gentleman Jim" Corbett (pro-cigarette and clean-shaven) knock out "The Boston Strong Boy" John L. Sullivan (anti-cigarette and moustachioed) for the Heavyweight title in 1892. And a Cigar Compromise: P. Lorillard brought out *Van Bibber* cigars—small, slim and cigarette-elegant—named after the debonair hero of the Richard Harding Davis stories.

James Buchanan Duke of American Tobacco, getting the drop on the Twentieth Century, went from tobaccoman to tobacco tycoon. His methods reflected the then-burgeoning practices of Morgan, Carnegie and Rockefeller whose management placed volume first and profits second. Meat packing, oil, whisky, copper, lead and lumber put the new machinery and volume practices to work to make big business, bigger trusts and eventual

Rex Mays, Roscoe Turner, Ducky Medwick, Tommy Farr, Clint Frank, Tailspin Tommy, Captain Tim, Ken Maynard, Count von Luckner, the Gee-Bee, Auburn Speedster, Riley's Sons of Notre Dame, Bill DeCorrevont, Jimmy Cagney, et al. And Boyhood Dreams Came True: an Indian summer's day lolled away in an Oxford Road backyard listening to Dick Powell and a sea-sick sax section chant "shipmates stand

monopolies. Duke had begun to diversify as early as 1891 with the purchase of the National Tobacco Works of Louisville, famous for its *Piper Heidsieck* plug tobacco. Other plug acquisitions followed: P. Lorillard, Marburg, Butler-Drummond-Brown, all funneled into a new corporation, The Continental Tobacco Company. A rival combine, the Union Tobacco Company headed by financiers Thomas Fortune Ryan, William C. Whitney, Anthony H. Brady and P. A. B. Widener, had bought out Duke's old rival Blackwell's *Bull Durham* and had an option on Liggett & Meyers, a St. Louis plug firm. In addition, Union had taken over an important cigarette firm—National Cigarette and Tobacco of New York. In 1899 the rival combines became one, bringing Duke some of the most powerful moneymen of the day. Later that year American Tobacco bought a two-thirds interest in a Winston-Salem plugmaker, R. J. "Josh" Reynolds, which Duke would hear from in the near future. Previously purchased P. Lorillard and Reynolds were allowed to operate more or less autonomously.

By the late 1890s cigarette sales had slumped back to the 1890 level. The cigarette tax was raised from 50¢ to $1.00 to $1.50 per thousand units to help pay for the Spanish-American War, and American Tobacco's nickel brands, like the best-selling Gay Nineties–named *Cycle,* couldn't hold the nickel price. Sales dropped from 600 million to 40 million units in two years. In 1902 the tax of $1.50 per thousand was lowered to 54¢ and sales turned upward.

While Duke and American Tobacco were buying out, jockeying, "trusting" and watching the tax levy go up and down, Greek, Turkish and Egyptian tobacconists in New York City were backroom rolling (as they had since Civil War times) all-Turkish smokes to the "festoon" of 750,000,000 cigarettes and a full twenty-five per cent of the market by 1903. All-Turkish had been

together, don't give up the ship" and Rudy Vallee telling us what college Betty Coed's lips are red for. Football dreams interrupted by golfers and duffers beating the brush behind the green adjacent to our "gridiron." And then a gruff "Didya see my ball kid?" as a white plus-foured Babe Ruth nimbly stepped over the rock wall onto our playing field. "Rushing the season, ain't you?" I knew it was Babe Ruth and

the "elegant smoking life" for the Carriage Trade, but had faded with the racial and immigrant slurs of the early Nineties. War correspondents Stephen Crane, Arthur Brisbane and Richard Harding Davis; and Guantanamo Bay, Aguinaldo, Manila, the Boxer Rebellion, the Klondike and Teddy Roosevelt at San Juan Hill would change all that! U.S. isolationism crumbled, and as America embraced a budding imperialism so New Yorkers embraced the romantic place names and "involvement" of all-Turkish cigarettes. Cigar store Indians went Turkish and so did American Tobacco!

American broadened its lines across the board! It leased or purchased the all-Turkish manufacturers M. Melachrino & Co., S. Anargyros, Monopol and Schinasi Brothers for their mostly expensive brands: *Egyptian Deities, Murad, Helmar, Mogul, Schinasi Natural, Egyptian Prettiest, Egyptian Straights* and *Melachrino.*

Prices ranged from the expensive *Egyptian Deities* and *Egyptian Prettiest* at 10 for 25¢ to the more competitive pricing of *Murad, Mogal* and *Schinasi Natural* at 10 for 15¢. *Helmar,* the cheapest all-Turkish smoke, was 10 for 10¢. Duke effected a Turkish compromise by blending the high-priced Turkish leaf with straight Virginia for the more nationwide smokes, *Hassan, Mecca* and *Fatima,* 10 for 5¢. American then brought out a new all-domestic, *Piedmont,* at 10 for 5¢ which competed with and soon passed its "standard for years," *Sweet Corporal.* American's cheapest brands—*American Beauty, Coupon, King Bee* and *Home Run*—were straight domestic and went at 20 for 5¢. Package design varied on the all-Turkish and Turkish blends according to price; but caliphs and harem beauties (reclining and unveiled on *Murad,* veiled and mysterious on *Fatima*), minarets and mosques were the exotic lures. Only *Hassan* was unadorned.

yet *I remember thinking of Wallace Beery and Victor McLaglen as my companion and I wished we had gloves and a bat. But the Babe autographed our upstart football in return for a bottle of Cott orange, and with laughs and curses went back to a new ball and a lie and a perfect chip to the pin! The Thirties ended with a two-week stay in Boy Scout Camp where mess was taken with unison singing of "A Big Bad Man*

A pink Eastern letter on a dark green background. Regular and slide-and-shell boxes said "cork tip or plain," "Push This End," "One Calls For Two" and "Valuable Coupon Enclosed." Virtually all domestic "cheapies" and Turkish blends had their cigarette trade cards. *Mecca's* "champion athlete and prize fighter series" were especially succinct—fighter's biography, date, opponent and decisions by round; baseball cards had number of games, at bats, batting average and fielding percentages. By 1904 American Tobacco had Turkish sales of over 400 million—about half the independents' total—domestic sales approaching the 3 billion mark and 88 per cent of the nation's cigarette industry.

But *Connorton's Tobacco Directory* for that year listed 2,124 "cigarettes, cigarros and cheroots." A "warren" of white rolls. Only the redoubtable *Bull Durham* stood out as a real American standard brand—"known the world over."

By the early 1900s "Hurry Up" America had a National Pastime! Baseball *was*—like the familiar tag line on advertising of the period—Everywhere! From the first World Series in 1903 to the Black Sox Scandal of 1919, baseball was a "Winesburg, Ohio" of prairie towns, Sally Leagues, spit-balls and firehouses—told by a Ring Lardner to a Booth Tarkington for the education of *Studs Lonigan* and *Penrod Schofield.* In the bleachers were the Standard Brands Generation to be—able to "Remember the Maine"; go to Yale with *Frank Merriwell;* trade an Eddie Cicotte and a Larry Doyle for a Smokey Joe Wood; whistle "In the Gloaming, Genevieve"; say "Uneeda Biscuit, Whoneeda Biscuit?"; and "Oh, Yeah!" to everything after 1920. They came to tobacco by way of the cigarette trade card, especially the baseball card, filched, begged and found in the gutter from their long-pants, "coffin-nail" seniors. Behind the gazebo, down by the railroad tracks, or any convenient "Old Ox Road" was spring

28

from Ok-la-homa" and a secret scout ritual—The Order of the Arrow —was supposed to fill our waking moments. I had the singing and the baseball and the "buddy" swims, and Penrod-style I sampled some of the Americana preludes to smoking. Cornsilk and Cubebs were passed around amid heated arguments as to the worthlessness of this "Sachem" and that "Sagamore." One older boy had the real thing—a

training for the "makin's" of cornsilk, hay-seed cigarettes, Cubebs and a courageously puffed *Sweet Caporal*. Some, like *Studs Lonigan*, would (with later rue) turn their backs forever on *Dink Stover, The Rover Boys, The Outdoor Chums, Tom Swift* and *The Boy Allies*, go through life with a cigarette "pasted in his mug." Of others—like William Sylvanus Baxter of Booth Tarkington's *Seventeen*—one couldn't be too sure: "However, having worn his tragic face for three blocks, he halted before a corner drug-store, and permitted his expression to improve as he gazed upon the window display of My Little Sweetheart All-Tobacco Cuban Cigarettes, the Package of Twenty for Ten Cents. William was not a smoker—that is to say, he had made the usual boyhood experiments, finding them discouraging; and though at times he considered it humorously man-about-town to say to a smoking friend, 'Well, I'll tackle one o' your ole coffin-nails,' he had never made a purchase of tobacco in his life. But it struck him now that it would be rather debonair to disport himself with a package of Little Sweethearts upon the excursion. And the name! It thrilled him inexpressibly.... He felt that when he should smoke a Little Sweetheart it would be a tribute to the ineffable visitor for whom this party was being given—it would bring her closer to him. His young brow grew almost stern with determination, for he made up his mind, on the spot, that he would smoke oftener in the future—he would become a confirmed smoker, and all his life he would smoke My Little Sweetheart All-Tobacco Cuban Cigarettes."

While across the land "little smokers" were in transit, and multiplying furiously, another big cigar smoker sat in the White House. Teddy Roosevelt and his Rough Riders had ridden "rough" but "slipshod" at San Juan Hill (it took an all-Negro outfit, the Tenth Cavalry, to win the day!) but Bully Teddy, *cellophane-wrapped package of Chesterfields with the matches inserted professionally under the wrapper. At night after taps he would run—cross-country style—the two miles to town and back for his secret pleasure. Tho not yet a smoker, I took to running with him those late summer nights, out of a sense of adventure and because I saw myself as a "Peck's Bad Boy" in revolt against the sadistic and hypo-*

politically exiled as Vice-President, was catapulted into the Presidency by the assassination of McKinley. For the next seven years the New York strong boy "Big Sticked" at home and abroad. "Walking softly" so that everyone could hear him coming, Roosevelt built the Panama Canal, mediated the Russo-Japanese War, intervened in Morocco between France and Germany, and sought to protect his gotten-gains abroad by urging a more powerful Navy. At home the "Big Stick" invoked the dusty Sherman Anti-Trust Act and clubbed coal, rail, oil, sugar and meat trusts. Teddy belabored forty-four major combines in all, foremost being James J. Hill and J.P. Morgan's Northern Securities Railroad combination and James Buchanan Duke's The American Tobacco Company.

In July, 1907, the U.S. Government brought suit against The American Tobacco Company for "combination in restraint of trade." The suit, begun by Roosevelt, was one of ninety such prosecutions pushed through by his successor, William Howard Taft, but it did not reach the Supreme Court until November, 1911. Duke himself drew up the plan for the spin-off, submitted to and approved by the Attorney General and published as a Court decree. The first great innovator of the tobacco industry soon left to become board chairman of British-American Tobacco, an independent subsidiary involved in the break-up.

The American Tobacco Company spin-off resulted in the formation of three new companies: Liggett & Myers, P. Lorillard and R. J. Reynolds. None of these companies was new, Lorillard and Reynolds having operated almost autonomously under Duke's wing, and *all* having existed as independents before Duke was in the cigarette business. P. Lorillard, founded in 1760, was the oldest and had seen the successive eras of tobacco history—pipe, snuff, chewing tobacco and the cigarette. Liggett & Myers and critical Golden Rule of the Boy Scouts of America. As an added thrill I would pocket the smokes on the run back to camp, feeling less "brave, clean and reverent." There was cigarette gossip in the seventh grade, that fall of Pearl Harbor, in which the more sophisticated members of the class were seen buying and smoking away from the school grounds. There was a notorious daughter of a Twenties society band

R. J. Reynolds were post-Civil War plugmakers from St. Louis and Winston-Salem. All had profited from the trust and one, "Josh" Reynolds, would get back at and use some of Duke's acumen to found a new and more revolutionary cigarette empire.

Liggett & Myers was given *Piedmont, Fatima, American Beauty, Home Run, Imperiales, Coupon* and *King Bee*—about 28 per cent of the cigarette market, the only 15¢ Turkish blend *(Fatima)* and the cheap straight domestic brands. P. Lorillard received *Helmar, Egyptian Deities, Turkish Trophies, Murad* and *Mogul*—15 per cent of the nation's business and *all* straight-Turkish brands. American Tobacco kept *Pall Mall,* its expensive all-Turkish brand, old standby *Sweet Caporal,* and *Hassan* and *Mecca,* its cheap Turkish blends, retaining 37 per cent of the market. R. J. Reynolds received no cigarette line but was awarded 20 per cent of the plug trade.

Cigarette sales had quadrupled from a fraction more than 3 billion units in 1904 to around 13 billion in 1912. The Turkish rush was slowing and nickel brands were holding their own, but there was an increase in the use of pipe tobacco blends and straight domestic *(Bull Durham)* by the large rural market which preferred the "roll-your-own" cigarette. The pipe was going out as the "contemplative" gave way to the "hurry up." It would remain as a "stance" in men's clubs and as a sign of "maturity" with sophomores, but its tobacco formula would thrust the cigarette into a new era of big, blended Standard Brands.

Once again, failure of a sort provided the impetus for an astounding success. The trust spin-off saw each company retrenching and filling the gaps in its cigarette lines—American with *Omar,* a high-priced Turkish blend; P. Lorillard with *Ziro* and *Nebo,* low-priced Turkish blends; Liggett & Myers testing a straight domestic, *Chesterfield;* and Reynolds trying cheap and *leader, a scion of a Coca-Cola billboard family, and a beauty of Turkish descent whose name rhymed with the cymbal-making family who had been Stork Clubbing that summer. They were all rich, or, if not rich, at least offspring of a family-style that refused to accept the grimness of the depression. They never got to high school. Many of our town's celebrity families moved northward to Connecticut that*

medium-priced Turkish blends, Reyno and Osman. Reynolds' Turkish blends rung up a "no sale." In desperation "R. J." turned to and adapted his most successful product—*Prince Albert* smoking tobacco. *Prince Albert,* introduced in 1907, was a granulated plug-cut smoking tobacco with a large percentage of flavored Burley leaf that did well in rural areas. Reynolds transferred the *Albert* formula—cased or sweetened Burley, a seasoning of Turkish, some Bright, flue-cured—and paper-and-foil wrapped a Barnum & Bailey dromedary belittling the Pyramids. He called it *Camel,* 20 for 10¢.

In 1914 "The Hump" was introduced with a $1,500,000 ad campaign: "The Camels are coming! Tomorrow there'll be more CAMELS in this town than in all Asia and Africa combined!" Almost true! By 1918 Camel had 40 per cent of the nation's cigarette business and was the No. 1 "Rose of No Man's Land."

Percival S. Hill became president of The American Tobacco Company upon the dissolution of the giant trust in 1912. Named to the post by the departing "Buck" Duke, Hill had come to American as manager of W. T. Blackwell's *Bull Durham* in the 1899 merger of Union Tobacco and American. He became vice-president in charge of sales and, in 1905, brought his twenty-five-year-old son, George Washington Hill, into the company as a trainee in the various tobacco markets. In 1907, on one of their acquisition sprees, American bought a New York firm—Butler-Butler—for their cigarette line of *Pall Mall, Egyptian Straights, Sovereign* and *Laurens.* The "two-seasoned" young Hill was put in charge and concentrated on one brand, *Pall Mall,* with a thinking and psychology that would characterize the Standard Brand era of a half dozen years later. Young Hill supervised and devised new wrinkles on all the variants that Major Ginter and Duke had started in the Eighties: premiums, trade cards, prize-

(Clockwise) *Sweet Caporal* or "Sweet Caps," an 1868 Kinney marque, were American Tobacco's "standard brand" straight Bright tobacco smokes of Granddad's day, ten for a nickel, in a slide-and-shell box. Studs Lonigan grew up on them and Garbo smoked them as she "talked" in the 1930 screen version of *Anna Christie*. American's cheap brands—*Home Run, Sunshine* and *Coupon*—went twenty for a nickel. *Home Run* and *Coupon* went to Liggett & Myers in the 1912 "Tobacco Trust" spin-off.

Cigar store Indians went Turkish; Potentates "potentated"; Harem beauties re-
clined; and cigarette ads ranged from *Murad's* "Be Nonchalant" to *Fatima's* "E
Sensible." By 1903 the Turkish cigarette boom had swept 25% of the market. Thes
smokes were all-Turkish or Balkan leaf, shorter and fatter, some ovaled, and most
hand-rolled. American Tobacco got in step and broadened its lines with the Turkis
Virginia blends of *Fatima* and *Mecca*—ten for a nickel; a more expensive all-Turkis

smoke, *Murad*—ten for fifteen and later twenty cents; and *Omar*, a high grade Turkish blend at twenty for fifteen cents. *Fatima* went to Liggett & Myers and *Murad* to Lorillard in the 1912 breakup of the American Tobacco Trust. American's subsidiary, Schinasi, sold the straight Turkish *Egyptian Prettiest* at twenty for thirty-five cents. Lorillard's *Mogul* was straight Egyptian at the same price.

CIGARETTE TRADE CARDS
1878-1940

Cigarette cards originated in the United States and Canada in the late 1870s as sales promotion devices and subject "enticements." Placed in each pack, cards reflected such diverse subject matter as (below, clockwise) *Mecca's* boxing and billiard series; *Fatima's* actress series; *Wills'* first aid course; and *Turf* cigarettes film stars. (At right) *Salem* of Dresden boosted Nazi Germany, and *Hassan* had auto drivers and ball players; *Sweet Caporal* had soubrettes.

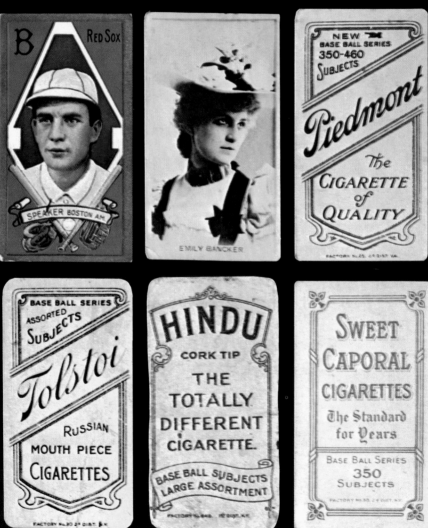

(Clockwise) "Tomorrow there'll be more CAMELS in this town than in all Asia and Africa combined!" R. J. Reynolds launched *Camels* in 1914 and began the era of the standard brands. Lorillard's *Old Gold* quickly established a share of the market in 1926 with its "Blindfold Test" campaigns. *Lucky Strike*, American's Burley blend, came out in 1917 and within the year had an 11% share of the market. Original *Herbert Tareyton* package dates from 1913 and was a Bright blend, no Burley.

n the summer of '31 Russ Columbo was singing *Please*, and *Lucky Strike* was saying "O.K. America." "Please" won out. Flue-cured leaf dropped from 19¢ to 12¢ per pound and Burley 25¢ to 11¢. Tobacco was not "depression-proof" and "ten-centers" appeared. Larus Brothers, Richmond, brought out *White Rolls*. Philip Morris introduced *Paul Jones*—"America . . . Here's your cigarette—20 for 10¢." Brown and Williamson reduced the price on *Wings*, and orders couldn't be filled fast enough.

REACH FOR A DIME INSTEAD OF FIFTEEN CENTS
1930-1940

Axton-Fisher, well established with the mentholated *Spud*, brought out *Twenty Grand* for a dime and by year's end "economy brands" had 25% of the domestic market. Other off-beat and regional brands were: (Above) Philip Morris' *Barking Dog*; Reed Tobacco's DC-3-packaged *Airline*; Lambert Pharmaceutical's *Listerine*; and (previous page) Lucky Strike's experimental (24 cigarettes for 15¢) *"111"* and Liggett & Myers southern regional, *Picayune*.

LUCKY STRIKE GREEN HAS GONE TO WAR
1940-1945

And so did Chesterfield, Camel, Old Gold and Philip Morris. World War II saw the emergence of cigarette rationing, and if our Marines in China were getting *Sensations, Dunhills* and *Fleetwoods* in their C rations, then what was to be had on the Home Front? (Clockwise) *Rum and Maple's* pouch tobacco gone cigarette; *Marvels*—a smattering Turkish blend; *Coffee-Tone*—another pouch tobacco extract; and *Raleigh*—Brown and Williamson's late Thirties "standard brand" entry.

Rule, Britannia! And smoke Virginia! Since the days of John Rolfe and Jamestown, the British have preferred the sweet and yellowed tobacco of Virginia and Maryland. (Top) Cork-tipped *Craven "A"*—"They never catch your throat." (Bottom) "Mummy's Favourite!"—John Player and Sons' *Player's Navy Cut,* cork-tipped and plain. Ian Fleming's *James Bond* detested these Virginia cigarettes and, as if in rebuke, was forever lighting a fortieth or fiftieth Macedonian.

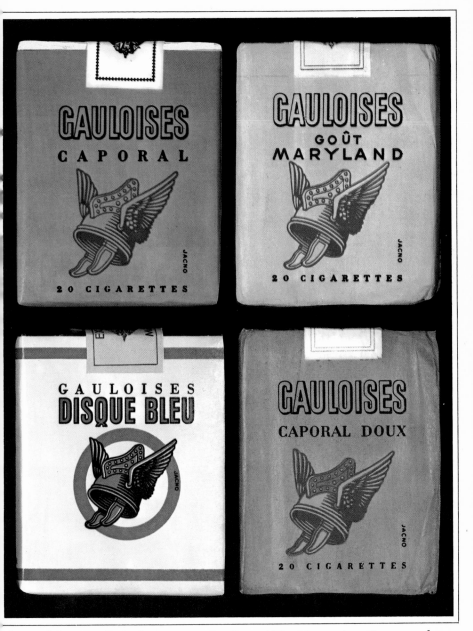

The Gauloises Family is the strongest family . . .! No. 1 in western Europe and now distributed in the U.S. by Philip Morris, Gauloises come in four blends: (Clockwise) *Gauloises Bleu*—loosely packed, straight Caporal, forever going out; *Gauloises Gout Maryland*—loosely packed, Virginia mix, forever going out; *Gauloises Disque Bleu* —loosely packed, milder, forever going out; and *Gauloises Caporal Doux*—loosely packed, Turkish mix, forever going out!

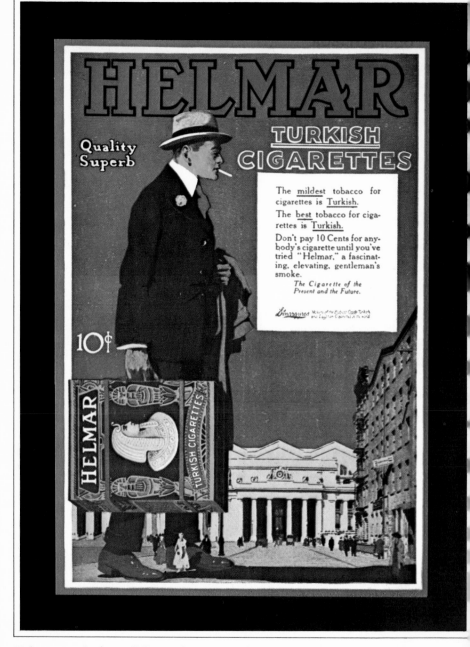

Helmar marched to a different drummer and went to Lorillard upon the dissolution of the American Tobacco Trust. Turkish sales had peaked by World War I, and ads in the Twenties took the "standard brands" approach; endorsements—"King Alfonso of Spain smokes Melachrinos"; and "think" campaigns—"Be Nonchalant, Light a Murad." But in 1916, *Helmar* (above) was stressing a "gentleman's smoke" in a format resembling a *Scribner's* or *Lippincott's* magazine cover.

A nickel more than *Helmar* at ten for fifteen cents, *Murad* was the volume leader among the more expensive all-Turkish cigarettes. Early ad copy stressed "wherever America's social life centers"—and Charles Dana Gibson–styled line drawings depicted Bailey's Beach and The Casino at Newport or a Four Hundred outing at the Vanderbilt Cup. By 1916, *Murad* (above) had gone color, and despite the line "Everywhere Why" was still big-city, Eastern and class-conscious.

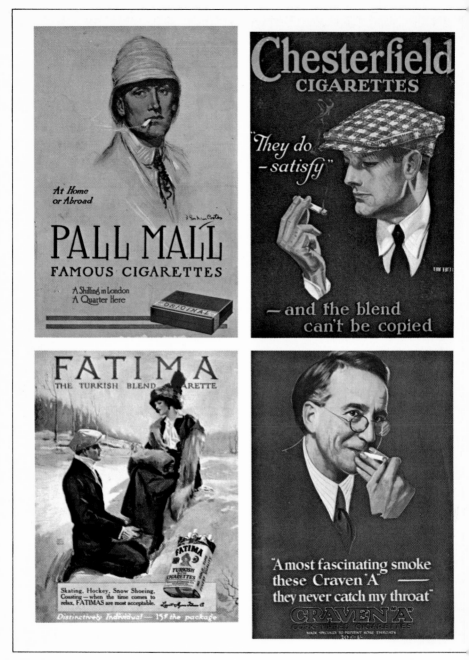

(Clockwise) Youthful ad man George Washington Hill made *Pall Mall*, straight Turkish until 1936, the volume leader in the 25¢ class with "firsts" like this 1916 magazine back cover. Test-marketed in 1912, *Chesterfield*—20 for 10¢—was Ligget & Myers' "big brand" blend with the stress on "satisfaction." *Craven "A"* was middle-class English and straight Virginia in 1927. *Fatima*—20 for 15¢—appealed to the outdoor man of 1915 and his sense of "relaxation."

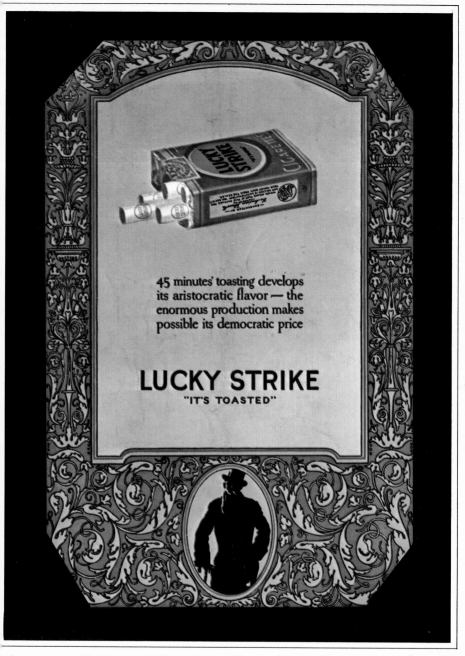

45 minutes' toasting develops
its aristocratic flavor — the
enormous production makes
possible its democratic price

LUCKY STRIKE
"IT'S TOASTED"

When George Washington Hill took over the presidency of American Tobacco in 925, his Burley favorite, *Lucky Strike*, was a poor third at 16% to *Chesterfield's* 24% nd *Camel's* 41% in the Big Three race. Still, a far cry and only 25 years from the ,000-odd "no brands" land of 1900. Hill retained Albert D. Lasker and his ad agency, ord & Thomas, and by 1929 could afford the beauty and the waste of the "soft sell" eprint (above) in *Vanity Fair*.

"Reach for a Lucky Instead of a Sweet" (bottom, right) broke in 1928, and by 193
Lucky Strike was No. 1. Hill and Lasker broke with tradition by using women—per
sonalities like aviatrix Amelia Earhart and actress Alice Brady—for testimonials i
the late Twenties and, (bottom, left) got around to "thank-you's" in 1932. Howeve
Howard Chandler Christy's 1933 illustration (top) was too subtle and too soft, an
Luckies began to lose ground to rivals *Chesterfield* and *Camel*.

year and their sons and daughters went off to boarding schools. By the fall of 1942 I was ripe for tracking down the spectre of cigarette-hood! And I thought I had a good reason. That summer, while listening to the Chicago Bear-College All-Star football game, I doubled up with pain and went to the hospital to have my appendix removed. When I got out that fall and entered high school I discovered that dur-

in-every-package, etc. But it was in the print ad with the psychological "copy lure" that George Washington Hill showed his early promise and through such ads that American Tobacco would one day swap and jockey for volume leadership. Hill started something new by advertising *Pall Mall* on magazine back covers: "At Home or Abroad. A Shilling in London, A Quarter Here" (a color illustration of a British colonial in topee hat). Hill's ad copy was as varied as the market expectation: a 1916 plea for renewed sales of *Sweet Caporals*—"Who smoked 'Sweet Caps' when Garfield and Hancock ran for President? Ask Dad, he knows"; on keeping *Mecca* in the vanguard of the low-priced Turkish rush—"TO ALL PEOPLE MECCA MEANS GOAL"; and to introduce *Omar,* a high-grade Turkish blend—"OMAR *OMAR* spells Aroma [salesman should here take his pencil and illustrate the trick]...Smoke Omar for Aroma." Hill's ad talents were also turned to the smoking tobacco business. For *Bull Durham*—" 'The Makings of a Nation'. You can make for yourself, with your own hands, the mildest, most fragrant cigarette in the world—and the most economical. Machines can't imitate it. The only way to get that freshness, that flavor, that lasting satisfaction is to 'roll your own' with good old 'Bull' Durham tobacco." And for *Tuxedo* smoking tobacco—"A Dash—of Chocolate." "Your Nose Knows."

By 1916 Hill had promoted and advertised his red-and-gold-boxed *Pall Mall* to the top of the 25¢ all-Turkish class. But it was not a volume market, and *everything* had begun to recede before "Josh" Reynolds' Burley-blended *Camel.* By 1915 Liggett & Myers had up-dated its slide-and-shell boxed test *Chesterfield* of 1912 to a paper-and-foil wrapped Turkish and American blend which took its place alongside *Camel* as the second of the Standard Brands. The trend was toward the big, Burley blends of *Camel*

ing the summer all my friends, it seemed everyone, had grown 4 to 6 inches! I went from a star cherry-hop-gobbling third baseman on the Grammar School Nine to a diminutive Studs Lonigan-type eighth-grader who quickly garnered the nickname "pusher"—to describe a newly found and necessary combativeness. Our high school fronted on twin lakes with a macadam causeway down the center. One side

and *Chesterfield,* and straight Turkish, Turkish blends and such domestic Brights as American's *Sweet Caporal* and Liggett's *Piedmont* were quickly beginning to fade. *Lucky Strike,* the third Standard Brand, would complete the revolution of the cigarette industry!

The name *Lucky Strike* derived from R. A. Patterson's pipe-smoking sliced plug, registered in 1871. Original design featured an arm-with-hammer which Patterson changed to a red bull's-eye on a blazing green background. Duke invested in the Patterson plug in 1903 and gained control in 1905. Hill worked on the new package design (paper-and-foil wrap) heavying up the "Lucky Strike" lettering in the bull's-eye, replacing the dimensional "sliced plug" with the word "cigarettes." On the back of the package was a smaller bull's-eye explaining the contents: "A BLEND *of* BURLEY *and* Turkish Tobacco *(based on the* ORIGINAL LUCKY STRIKE TOBACCO FORMULA). An entirely NEW principle in cigarette manufacture. 'IT'S TOASTED'."

"It's toasted" became the handle (actually referring to the cooking process involved), and the first black-and-white ads (designed for newspapers) appeared in January, 1917, with the *Lucky Strike* package on a slant and at the left a bull's-eye showing a piece of toast being held by a fork over a fire. Hill would vary the toast idea later with steak and even potatoes! By 1918 Luckies were pushing the 6 billion mark, about 11 per cent of cigarette sales. In the spring of 1918 the U.S. Government contracted for the entire output of *Bull Durham,* and the "makin's" went overseas to the Doughboys—complete with copy: "When our boys light up, the Huns will light out!"; "The Makings for US, The Leavings for the Kaiser!" With Pershing calling for smokes and more smokes, caliphs and harem beauties (reclining and unveiled on *Murad,* veiled and mysterious on *Fatima*), *of the lake was fringed with a still-ample covering of bullrushes where, during several lunch hours, my Cigarette Fagin and his pupils repaired for what was to be my "baptism by smoke." Chesterfields again. There was something mild even about the package compared with the more tobacco-colored design of Camels and the graphic warning of the Lucky Strike bull's-eye. Chesterfields looked mild and harm-*

minarets and mosques also went overseas to the trenches and served many a "lucifer" with a smile! *They* never did come back!

The Standard Brands Generation was no longer in the bleachers! World War I had seen to that! They would return to May Day riots and then welcome President Harding's "normalcy." Spiritually tired, they wanted a "peace of one's own" and so would embark on Scott Fitzgerald's "greatest, gaudiest spree in history."

The dance of the last cigarette which began when I was twenty has not reached its last figure yet. My resolutions are less drastic and, as I grow older, I become more indulgent to my weaknesses. When one is old one can afford to smile at life and all it contains. I may as well say that for some time past I have been smoking a great many cigarettes and have given up calling them the last.
—Italo Svevo,
CONFESSIONS OF ZENO, 1930

oodbye *black* and hello *blue*" colors the spectrum of the Roaring Twenties! *Black* was Victorian. *Black* was the failed idealism of Wilson's gleaming topper. *Black* was the "Say it ain't so, Joe" of the Black Sox Scandal! And *black,* as in blackbird, was what one said "Bye, Bye" to. Everyone under thirty was "Blue Again" now and then, but most said "My Blackbirds Are Bluebirds Now," and some "There's A Bluebird On My Shoulder"—but all said "Bye, Bye, Blackbird!" Some Flappers and Whoopee Mamas had a "My Blue Heaven" while others became "Little Girl Blue" because they were "True Blue Lou!"

The philosophy of Popular Songs, and the belief in them, hovers over the New Morality of the Twenties. From "Flaming Youth" to "Wall Street Wail," in tempo or lyric, Rodgers & Hart, Cole Porter, Jerome Kern, Arthur Schwartz, Richard Whiting, Kalmar & Ruby, DeSylva, Brown & Henderson, Irving Berlin, Duke Ellington, Noel Coward and Fats Waller brought a précis of intelligibility that was almost literature. "Bye, Bye, Blackbird," a rueful lament in the guise of a peculiarly American "stiff upper lip," was the "standard-bearer" of a generation that had "fought all wars . . ."

The Jazz Age found heady particles of truth in its songs—that business could be reduced to a banal wisecrack ("Yes, We Have No Bananas"); that staying up and out late had its advantages ("Three O'clock in the Morning," "Last Night on the Back Porch"); that some couples wanted to settle down ("The Love Nest," "Cottage Small by a Waterfall") and reiterate their fidelity ("Ain't Misbehavin'," "No One Else but You"), and that other couples were *worried* about fidelity ("Save It Pretty Mama"); that some people yearned to be where they weren't ("Avalon," "Georgia On My Mind," "There's a Cabin in the Pines"); that love's maltreatment could be fun ("You Took Advantage of Me")

less and didn't "they satisfy" according to all the advertisements? Those long lunch hours became a gauntlet of all the smoker's tricks, affectations and pleasures. There were: smoke rings without inhaling (the correct way); smoke rings with inhaling, the ring being made out of the exhale (difficult); French Inhaling (which I practiced but couldn't master); lighting two cigarettes at once—one for your girl,

and that love's maltreatment could hurt ("Mean to Me," "Who's Sorry Now?," "After You've Gone"), and that love's old sweet song could be a new song ("Can't We Be Friends?"). That luck had a lot to do with it ("I'm Looking Over a Four Leaf Clover"), or that luck had nothing whatsoever to do with it ("There'll Be Some Changes Made," "From Monday On"), and finally that for every "Everything Is Hotsy Totsy Now" there was a "Nobody's Sweetheart."

The automobile was all-pervasive in the Jazz Age. In silent films, as in real life, it was by turns an erotic arena, a harbinger of gangster wrath, a conveyance for Dancing Mothers and Dancing Daughters and the one industry crucial to American Business. The cigarette, on the other hand, became a character "prop" in film and literature. The films of the Jazz Decade, backed by a Wall Street republicanism, portrayed the New Morality in terms of the new consumer ethos. On the surface the Hollywood comedies, dramas and gangster films included all the new social and moral standards of the Jazz Age: the emancipation of American women, the breakdown of ethics and the old codes, a Freudian fascination with sex, the new working girl and a sometime redefining of marital status. Visually, the selling props of American life were all there: short skirts and cigarette holders, bobbed hair and country clubs, ballrooms, speakeasies, cocktail parties and extravagant modern decor. But Hollywood, exercising its early double-think, made all the errant Flappers, It-Girls, Sheiks, and of course Business Johnnies, come home to roost—and like it! The dénouement was always middle class!

The cigarette often signified villainy and *too much* It-Girlishness. Erich von Stroheim used it stylishly to round out his portrayals of sadism and lechery in *Foolish Wives* and *Blind Husbands*. The height of cigarette villainy occurred in Percival Chris-

like Paul Henreid, or was it Bogart? for Bette Davis in "Now, Voyager"; the different methods of lighting a match against the wind; the one-handed strike, light and match-discard; the thumbnail—stick match light; the correct way to flip a "butt" and field-strip a cigarette; how to save the "long ones"; rolling Bull Durham; how to talk with a cigarette in your mouth without choking; the "Russian held" smok-

topher Wren's beau gallant novel of the Jazz Age, *Beau Geste*. Wren's story of romance, intrigue and adventure was set in the Foreign Legion and opened with the discovery of a desert fort manned only by dead legionnaires. A flashback to the England of twenty years before, and to the childhood and code of the *Geste* brothers, showed an Edwardian love of England and mother, and the mysterious disappearance of a fabulous jewel. The brothers go their various ways and then find themselves in the Legion together, fighting not only the Arabs, but their villainous commanding officer, *Lejaune*. The fort comes under attack and *Digby* and *Michael Geste* are killed, their bodies hoisted into the embrasures, with rifles at ready to draw the Arab fire. Only *John Geste* and a few men are left, along with the sadistic *Lejaune:* "By Lejaune's orders, Vogue, in the dusk before moonrise, pushed the bodies of Schwartz, Haff, and Delarey from the look-out platform to fall down the roof. They were then posed in embrasures, as though living defenders of the fort. It seemed to give Lejaune special pleasure to thrust his half-smoked cigarette between Schwartz's teeth, and pull the dead man's *kepi* rakishly to one side. 'There, my fine conspirator,' said he when the body was arranged to his liking. 'Stand there and do your duty satisfactorily for the first time in your life, now you're dead. Much more useful now than ever you were before.' " In the 1927 silent film version, Ronald Colman played *Beau* and Noah Berry, Sr., played the evil *Lejaune*. William Wellman's exact talkie remake, 1939, had Gary Cooper as *Michael "Beau" Geste* and Brian Donlevy as *Lejaune*.

John Held's flapper had a "cigarette and a small red hat" when she left home "under a cloud!" *(Make my bed and light the light, I'll arrive, late tonight...)* It wasn't always that way! In 1882 Oscar Wilde and Lily Langtry arrived in New York, and they were *ing style; the cigarette-held-in-the-teeth style; the "butt" behind the ear, either as a "save" or a make-ready for the next smoking break; and where to carry your cigarettes—usually in you left-hand shirt pocket, especially if you were wearing a sweater as a cover-up, but never in your side pants pocket unless you had a plastic cigarette case; and lastly, the cover-up—the Sen-Sen, pumice stone and Wimpy-*

smoking. Cigarettes! Wilde was on the first of his lecture tours and Miss Langtry was appearing in *As in a Looking Glass*. Later that year Lily Langtry was photographed smoking a cigarette! And New Yorkers acted like Frenchmen. "Look, she's going to smoke!" drew nary a ripple of surprise. Lily was "of the theater," and theater people were allowed—for the pleasures they gave under the lights—their doctrine of indulgences, at least in the big cities. In New York, errant Carriage Trade daughters and even their mothers were known to indulge in the "novelty," acquired on the Continent through a succession of Grand Tours. London tobacconist and manufacturer Philip Morris had catered to the "ladies of the evening" and the Music Hall with an 1889 ad: "Cork Tipped Cigarettes are a luxury to the lips." The ad illustration showed a multi-petticoated girl with skirt pulled over the calves, smoking and perched on a "cork tip." It would be almost 45 years before George Washington Hill would be the "first" to use a girl with a cigarette in an American ad campaign. In the Nineties, home-grown but forever-after-wandering Lola Montez—actress, courtesan and former mistress of the King of Bavaria—returned to New York and shocked New York *Herald* reporters with the statement that "she smoked 500 cigarettes a day!" Though she was in her mid-fifties by then, a reporter wryly observed that smoking had made "inroads on her beauty."

The "hurry up" beginnings of the Twentieth Century saw *more* American girls smoking clandestinely! Suffrage was a part of it, but the Shop Girl "lunch pail" was a greater part! It took the new freedom of the automobile and *somewhere* to go in it, however, to bring cigarette smoking out into the open for the young ladies-to-be of the Standard Brands Generation. In recognition, *Life* magazine, August 3, 1911, ran their Nicotine Number, with a cover illustration of a diapered baby girl smoking sized hamburgers smothered in onions, devoured at the all-night diner before returning home. *Those early years of smoking depended, somewhat unconsciously, on the styles and models of a Hollywood often glimpsed years before our habit: Cops-and-robbers, with the robber— twin stick matches in his teeth—emulating Leo Gorcey as the poker- playing "Spit" with Billy Halop and Bogart in "Dead End"; a bellig-*

one of her mother's cigarettes, titled "My Lady Nicotine."

Irene and Vernon Castle were responsible for "that somewhere to go" in the automobile. Their invented and popularized dance steps — "Castle Walk," "Turkey Trot" and the "Tango" — launched the Ballroom, Speakeasy and Roadhouse dance craze of the Twenties. Their own *Castle Gardens* out on Long Island pre- dated the great Roadhouses of the Twenties—*Gedney Farms* in Westchester, *Ross Fenton Farms* across the ferry in New Jersey, and *Longue Vue* near Harmon-on-the-Hudson. Before our entry into World War I, New York City had tea-and-after danc- ing in a score of famous spots: *Reisenweber's Cafe, Bustanoby's, Rector's, Shanley's, Moulin Rouge, Palais Royal* and *Churchill's* above Times Square.

Irene Castle cut her hair to start the bobbed-hair fashion which in a few years would spread the look of the Twenties; grand- mothers threw away their crutches to Turkey Trot; and wealthy juveniles by 1915 had discovered that petting, smoking and drinking in the seclusion of the family car could be the most exciting thing "ever." The New Morality was in its infancy, but with the publication of F. Scott Fitzgerald's *This Side of Paradise* in 1920 it was articulated: "Amory saw girls doing things that even in his memory would have been impossible, eating three- o'clock, after-dance suppers in impossible cafés, talking of every side of life with an air half of earnestness, half of mockery, yet with a furtive excitement that Amory considered stood for real moral let-down. But he never realized how wide-spread it was until he saw the cities between New York and Chicago as one vast juvenile intrigue."

The winning of the Suffrage and Volstead Acts — the drying out of America—both in 1920, coincided with the Birth of the Roaring Twenties! A man in the Polo Grounds dropped dead as *erent Mickey Rooney being relieved of his cigarette by a back-hand slap from Spencer Tracy in "Boys' Town"; and Henry Fonda and the smokes taken "on the lam" in Fritz Lang's "You Only Live Once." We tended to identify with the underdog and the smoking style of the rebel, and in Hollywood wasn't the criminal (read victim/rebel) getting his just deserts to placate the Hays Office? No wonder the tight*

Babe Ruth hit his forty-third homer of the season; Jack Dempsey stood trial as a draft dodger and beat the rap; Charles Chaplin made The Kid with Jackie Coogan; and H. L. Mencken attacked the business community: "The first Rotarian was the first man to call John the Baptist Jack." The idea of New Freedom for singles as well as the marrieds was espoused by heroine *Carol Kennicott* in Sinclair Lewis's *Main Street* of that year: "Solitary dishing isn't enough to satisfy me—or many other women. We're going to chuck it. We're going to wash 'em by machinery, and come out and play with you men in the offices and clubs and politics you've cleverly kept for yourselves!" The New Morality, said Scott Fitzgerald, had found "All gods dead, all wars fought, all faiths in man shaken." In revolt against their elders, the Younger Generation would take things into their own hands. They did. They were burnt out by 1923! Their elders, watching enviously in the wings, took over with the tabloid newspaper, Wall Street's invasion of Hollywood, and merchandising and advertising to boom the orgy of the Jazz Age for another half a decade.

Scott Fitzgerald's Depression essay "Echoes of the Jazz Age" characterized the prosperity of the Twenties: "It was an age of excess...the whole upper tenth of a nation living with the insouciance of grand ducs and the casualness of chorus girls." Henry Ford's streamlined production methods were partially responsible, but it was Albert D. Lasker and his advertising agency Lord & Thomas—through "Reason Why" salesmanship and advertising techniques—that taught the nation to consume out of all proportion to its needs. An orgiastic consumption of cars, clothes, radios, houses and home appliances could be attributed to Lasker's success with *Kleenex, Pepsodent, Quaker Oats* and *Frigidaire*. The advertising and selling of products was *inhale of Bogart and the jaunty, staccato drags of Cagney (we forgave him his turncoat "G-Man" role) infiltrated our consciousness. Later, upon cigarette maturity, some of us would more consciously incorporate the raffiné style of Adolph Menjou, Herbert Marshall, Cary Grant and William Powell. But the prime influence on my cigarette style in those early high school years under college-like spires, slates*

considered a patriotic duty, as were the ad-fostered Epicurean needs of the consumer; and nowhere was the temporal quality of products more in evidence than in the Hollywood silent-film comedies of Mack Sennett's Keystone Cops and Laurel & Hardy, with their frenzy of consumer product destruction. Millions laughed and not one "sat down and cried" as cars, clothes and appliances became grisly "grist" for the laugh mill. For the most powerful nation on earth and for Americans, "every day in every way grew better and better."

Things were growing "better and better," but not fast enough for George Washington Hill and his all-attention-getting favorite, *Lucky Strike*. American Tobacco was the last of the Big Three to make a blended, Standard Brand entry on the market, and the company was still in the process of changing over from the tobacco markets of the prewar era to the "concentration" of the one big cigarette! Hill and Lucky Strike even took to the air in 1923 with a skywriting campaign that saw 122 cities from coast to coast "rubbernecking" a three-mile-long "Lucky Strike" spelled out at 10,000 feet. However, 1925 "stats" showed Luckies a lean third at 13 billion units, behind the 20 billion of *Chesterfield* and the 34 billion unit sales of *Camel*. "Buck" Duke and Percival Hill died that year, and George Washington Hill became president of American Tobacco. Immediately Hill hired Albert Lasker and Lord & Thomas and began an assault on *Camel* sales.

By the mid-Twenties millions of American women were either smoking or affecting the cigarette as a Flapper "prop"! But no cigarette campaign had yet dared to come right out and testify that American women were smoking. Hill and Lord & Thomas decided not to hedge. They went out and got testimonials from actresses Alice Brady and Constance Talmadge and aviatrix Amelia Earhart. They also sought the personalities of the stage, *and gables, were the tough Irish, Italian and Negro youths. Smokers all! "Townies" most all! The Irish stand out—Episcopalian Irish or first-generation Wasp—a combination of the fictional Studs Lonigan and the biographical Scott Fitzgerald. They had the cigarette style, the athletic style and the "make-out" style. They were not "jocks" in the sense of being anti-intellectual, and, in fact, their imagination often*

screen, Broadway and the Golden Age of Sports—Al Jolson, Walter Hagen, John Gilbert, George Gershwin! The copy line was Hill's: "Reach for a *Lucky*—instead of a sweet"! The campaign broke in 1928 with three basic layouts—a black-and-white format for newspapers: "I light a *Lucky* and go light on the sweets. That's how I keep in good shape and always feel peppy" —signed Al Jolson. "Reach for a *Lucky* instead of a sweet" was not used as a headline on newspaper ads but appeared as an isolated copy spot. The two-color layouts were graphically handsome. One series had the look of a Saturday Evening Post cover. The "Reach for a *Lucky*" headline was at the top and bracketed by bold rules, while a silhouette, head and shoulders illustration of the stage or screen star floated in "white space" underneath. Testimonial copy was brief: "Luckies are the 'stars' of the cigarette picture"—signed John Gilbert, celebrated Screen Star. The other color format had a black-and-white line cartouche oval in which a color illustration of Amelia Earhart looked like a face at a porthole. The testimonial was more prominent: "Lucky Strikes were the cigarettes carried on the 'Friendship' when she crossed the Atlantic"—signed Amelia Earhart. "For a slender figure— Reach for a *Lucky* instead of a sweet" was much less conspicuous at the bottom of the ad.

Although Hill's headline was not original (in 1891, Lydia Pinkham had urged women to "Reach for a *vegetable* instead of a sweet") its stunning effect caused a furore among confectioners. Some stores, such as Schrafft's in New York, took Luckies off their counters, and the candy industry complained to the Federal Trade Commission. The FTC warned Hill that "cigarettes can't be sold as reducing devices." Hill, Lasker and the lawyers went back to the drawing board and came out with a new and hardly less effective campaign for 1929. The objection-

led to their athletic downfall. They would "dog it" in football or basketball practice, needling, joking, looking for some dramatic escapade to make light of their considerable gifts. They all belonged to the same fraternity and wore tan sweaters with orange and black V-neck stripes. They were always seen in clusters of three or four sweaters, verbally scuffling, their cigarettes mocking then enlightening. Most

able word "sweet" was dropped and a new headline and visual were drawn up. Illustrated silhouettes of trim athletes running, jumping, diving and followed by obese doubles in the same position. Copy read: "When tempted to over-indulge, reach for a Lucky instead." "Be moderate—be moderate in all things, even in smoking. Avoid that future shadow* by avoiding over-indulgence, if you would maintain that modern, ever-youthful figure." An asterisk note appeared at the bottom of all ads:"*We do not say smoking *Luckies* reduces flesh. We do say when tempted to over-indulge,'Reach for a *Lucky* instead'." By 1930 Lucky Strike was at the head of the pack, surpassing *Camel* with 42 billion in unit sales!

Although it was the age of the Standard Brand, Hill didn't neglect his other cigarettes' markets. By 1924 *Bull Durham* was in eclipse and the old nickel-a-sack price was raised to 2 bags for 15¢. An ad in *Judge* magazine was headlined: "100 cigarettes for 15¢." A Yale "clean-up" hitter was shown rolling. Either the bags had increased in size or the rolling had been streamlined (a nickel sack in the hands of a skilled roller produced around thirty-three smokes). That same year saw American's straight Turkish brand, *Pall Mall,* go into a standard size to get some volume market business: "53 inches of Turkish cigarette satisfaction—The new size PALL MALLS—20 for 30¢"(*Pall Mall* Regular, King Size at 85 and 90 millimeter, were still sold). A James Montgomery Flagg illustration appealed to "that easy chair hour when every man feels entitled to life's best."

George Washington Hill's advertising and promotional philosophy was: "I believe in merchandising in the flow of the stream ...I don't like to sell horse shoes and buggy whips. I like to sell what is growing; then it is more easy for me to get my share of what is growing." Hill "saw what was growing" in the contem-

were to go off to war in a few years and hardly any would distinguish themselves in college or beyond, but for those few years they were the White Hipsters of my cigarette youth. Lucky Strike Green had gone to war and, it seemed, half the world followed! There were servicemen everywhere! Where there's war there's smoke, and there was plenty of both on Swing Street—52nd Street in New York City—with its narrow

porary scene. His ad campaigns showed a sophisticated knowledge of his time. The "Reach for a *Lucky*" campaign took into consideration the popularity of Bernarr MacFadden's *Physical Culture* magazine, and the anxiety of a nation too rich and fat and worried about it—or, as Fitzgerald remembers: "...one day in 1926 we looked down and found we had flabby arms and a fat pot and couldn't say boop-boop-a-doop to a Sicilian." In direct contrast to Hill and *Lucky Strike, Camel* and *Chesterfield* "walked a mile" and "satisfied" right through the Twenties and into the Thirties without tapping the women's smoking market, the "star" testimonial, or any realities of the day. *Camels'* masculinity campaign and their trademark—"I'd walk a mile for a Camel"—persisted through the Twenties; and a woman wouldn't be recognized in their ads till a mid-Thirties comic-strip football sequence in which Coach Chick Meehan coached and coaxed "Betty and Bob" into the stadium to "light up" while they watched the game. *Chesterfield* came close in 1931 with a great headline—"Blow some my way." But poor layout and confusing body copy (a Depression psychology of better times?)—"Memories of a night in June...not so many years ago...and now, as then, Chesterfield's fragrance plays the same part in appealing to good taste "—reduced the effectiveness of a potentially fine ad campaign.

In the midst of Hill's sales battle with *Camel* and *Chesterfield,* P. Lorillard was preparing *its* Standard Brand entry. Lorillard had acquired *only* straight Turkish brands from the American Tobacco Trust spin-off and stayed Oriental until well after World War I! *Murad,* its volume leader, had a successful postwar "think" campaign based on the psychology of the "wallflower" or the socially ill-at-ease. "Why Be Embarrassed! Be Nonchalant—Light a *Murad!*" One particular advertisement il-

cellar boîtes lined with servicemen, where the dense smoke was cleaved by the vying Boppers Fats Navarro and Alan Eager at Clark Monroe's "Downbeat"; where an aching-hearted Billie Holiday commandeered a "hush" at the "Spotlight"; Jack Teagarden and his Candy Kids (members of the Scarsdale Hot Club) blew for the prep-school record collectors at "The Famous Door"; and the Dizzy Gillespie-

lustrated a cushion-reclining Harem Beauty (not smoking) compromised by a Flapper's "bee stung" lips and penciled eyebrows. It was in great contrast to the copy line and visuals of 1916 that had depicted a gowned lady and tuxedo-clad gentleman riding a magic carpet cigarette to some Vernon Castle ballroom for a Tango or a Turkey Trot. "Everywhere—Why?" was a copy fib as *Murad* was still big-city, Eastern and class-conscious.

Lorillard, like *Murad*, stayed nonchalant until 1925 sales figures showed that *Camel, Chesterfield* and *Lucky Strike* had captured some 81 per cent of unit sales! *Old Gold,* derived from an earlier Lorillard tobacco blend, became a Standard Brand entry in early 1926. *Old Gold* went Hill and Lasker one better with massive consumer testing in a "Double Blindfold Campaign." In the first testing several different blends were distributed—some of Lorillard's mixtures and some of the Big Three, all rolled in unmarked cigarette paper and unmarked boxes, but Lorillard-keyed. Samples were handed out across the country, and asked-for reports showed that a Lorillard blend was the most popular with the consumer. The chosen blend, named *Old Gold* after the Virginia Golden Belt tobacco country, was packaged with red lettering on a golden-yellow background showing scattered "Pieces of Eight" and the copy: "The Treasure of Them All."

The real "Blindfold Test" campaign began as smokers were asked to try each of four cigarettes—*Old Gold* and the three leading Standard Brands—with their brand names concealed by a wrapper: "Which cigarette *is really the most appealing?*" Reports from polled hotels and restaurants endorsed *Old Gold* as the most often chosen, and the resultant publicity was enough to launch the fourth Standard Brand. With the surge and mass dominance of the Big Three blends and their milder leaf, more smokers were inhaling and more smokers were coughing! On

Oscar Pettiford band were making Modern Jazz History at the "Onyx." The wartime "butt" allowed us to look older, even feel older, and we promised the bouncer a private detective at the door (after slipping him $2.00 apiece) that we wouldn't drink but had come to smoke in "self-defense" and listen to the jazz. Once inside it was always "what'll-youhave," and during that period if you could reach the bar you could

every print ad and billboard *Old Gold* stated: "Not a Cough in a Carload!" and sometimes added the tag "Not a Bark in a Billion!"

Old Gold's most successful print campaign of the Twenties utilized woodcut engravings by John Held, Jr., in a 1914 *Perils of Pauline* serial style: " 'TOOT! TOOT! IT'S THE EXPRESS. WILL YOU YIELD OR BE GROUND BENEATH THE WHEELS?' ROARED INGLESBY. 'Never!' cried our Nell, bound to the rails, her eyes blazing with defiance. 'Death is preferable to a life with such as you.' 'How do you make that out?' he purred. 'A rasping voice such as yours would make life a living hell,' she answered him. 'Unbind me, change to OLD GOLDS and maybe I'll listen to reason.' NOT A COUGH IN A CARLOAD! FASTEST GROWING CIGARETTE IN HISTORY!" Other print campaigns featured a Robert Ripley "Believe It Or Not" series and the first comic-strip cigarette campaign—*Ain't It a Grand and Glorious Feelin'?* by Briggs. *Old Gold* went on coast-to-coast radio in 1928 with "King of Jazz" Paul Whiteman and his retinue of Bix Beiderbecke, Frank Trumbauer, Eddie Lang, and The Rhythm Boys featuring Bing Crosby. Blanket advertising and personalized selling gave the newest Standard Brand 5 per cent of unit sales by the mid-Thirties.

By 1928 the coffers were full! There were two Houses of Morgan—one for J. P. and one for Helen! Mary Louise Cecilia Guinan—"Texas" to everyone but the Feds—wore a gold police whistle around her neck to mock the Prohibition agents who tried to keep up with the proliferation of Texas Guinan Clubs. Eddie Cantor's big hit "Makin' Whoopee" swept the country, and, not to be outdone, Montgomery Ward went from 117 to 440 while R.C.A. went from 85 to 420. Head waiters and barbers retired on a half-million won in the market! Cigarette unit sales went over the 122 billion mark, Americans bought over $850

get served. Intermissions were spent at the White Rose Bar on Sixth Avenue "catching" our favorite musicians and their "sharp" clothes. Later that year the Double-Breasted, one-button roll Chalk-Stripe Suit, the Barney Brooks roll-collar shirt, the bold-print Windsor-knotted tie and the heavy brogues became our "closet suit" to be worn weekly to "The Street." All of a sudden the big Name Brand cigarettes became

million worth of radios, and there were 23 million cars on the road. Calvin Coolidge wanted a Summer White House, to escape the heat in Washington; in New York the heat was being put on Mae West's latest, *Pleasure Man*. Vina Delmar's *Bad Girl* was a best-seller, and in Hollywood Joan Crawford was the latest, but not the last of, *Our Dancing Daughters*.

Everywhere there was a bloated, rich, "Oh, Yeah" *ennui*. The Spring and Summer of 1929 did repeat business. John J. Raskob of General Motors said: "Everybody Ought to Be Rich." The National Association of Merchant Tailors said that the average American male should have 20 suits, a dozen hats, 8 overcoats and 24 pairs of shoes! And for the *rich:* Black, Starr and Frost advertised in the New Yorker—"This necklace is conceded by experts and connoisseurs to be the finest in existence...Price $685,000."

Mark Twain thought that October was the cruelest month! In *Pudd'nhead Wilson* he states: "October. This is one of the peculiarly dangerous months to speculate in stocks. The others are July, January, September, April, November, May, March, December, August and February." Twain was right the first time! Black Wednesday became Black Thursday and Black Thursday became Black Tuesday, October 29, 1929. The greatest of all selling waves saw the 16 million shares traded set off a panic that destroyed 30 billion in market value. All went down from romantic Goldman, Sachs to the lowliest shopkeeper. In the wake of "Shoot me, for the love of God, someone shoot me," there appeared the suicide jokes. Hotel clerks queried: "You want a room for sleeping or jumping?" "Laughing At Life" had been replaced by the "Wall Street Wail," which gave way to "Blue Turning Grey Over You!" Flaming Youth and Whoopee Mama became Apple Al and Apple Annie, patrolling opposite street corners, within smoking distance of each other!

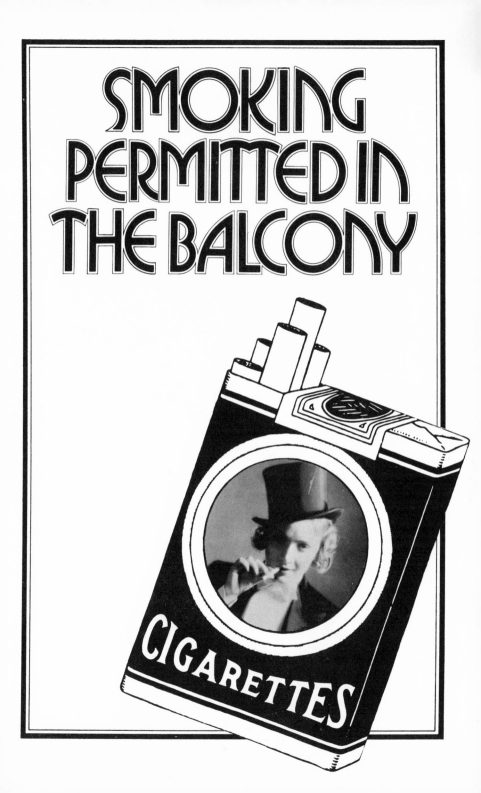

At the time of writing MY CIGARETTE LADY, I was undecided whether she should be the girl he had known—loved and lost—or the girl he hoped to meet, and whose face seemed to be in every cloud of smoke from his cigarette. I decided upon the latter, and this is the story, in song, of the girl he hopes to meet . . . I hope you like it.

—Rudy Vallee,
  MY CIGARETTE LADY, 1931

The Last Cigarette Generation was born to *Lucky Strike* saying "O.K. America" and Little Round Herbert Hoover saying "nobody goes hungry." A maturing and cynical Tin Pan Alley chipped in with "Life Is Just a Bowl of Cherries," "Wrap Your Troubles in Dreams" and "Dip Your Brush in the Sunshine" *(And Keep on Painting Away)*. Meanwhile the whole country was in drydock and the Ladder of Success had to be revised. Men who only a week before had approved your bank loan were suddenly shoveling snow or stumbling from door to door with encyclopedias! Tin Pan Alley became more accommodating with "Time on My Hands," "Shanty in Old Shanty Town" and "Brother, Can You Spare a Dime?"

The cock-eyed optimism of 1931 found Eddie Cantor singing "Potatoes are Cheaper—Tomatoes are Cheaper" *(Now's the Time to Fall in Love")* and several tobaccomen decided (since flue-cured leaf had dropped from 19¢ to 12¢ per pound, Burley from 25¢ to 11¢) that *cigarettes* could be cheaper! (Standard Brands were 20 for 15¢, some, like *Camel*, 2 packs for 25¢.) In the Fall of '31, Larus Brothers, Richmond, a regional firm, brought out *White Rolls* at 20 for 10¢. The next month, Prexy Reuben M. Ellis of Philip Morris & Co., Ltd., Inc. (by now an American corporation) announced *Paul Jones:* "America . . . Here's your cigarette—20 for 10¢." The new "economy" brands, or "ten-centers," really picked up when Brown & Williamson reduced the price on their Twenties brand *Wings* to 20 for 10¢ and Axton-Fisher of Louisville came out with Triple Crown–Winner *Twenty Grand*, a brand-new cigarette, at 20 for 10¢. By year's end the "economy rush" had 25 per cent of the domestic market. "Reach for a dime . . . instead of fifteen cents" was what a lot of Brothers did!

Almost as many Brothers reached for a nickel sack of *Bull Durham*. American Tobacco's *Bull* hadn't fit in with the Jazz

hard to get, except through a serviceman or a PX connection, and eventually became rationed. United Cigar, Whelan's and small candy stores became a repository for Coffee-Tone, Marvels, Wings, Fleetwood, Dunhill, Sensation, Twenty Grand, Fatima, Sunshine, Avalon, Johnnie Walker, English Ovals, Lord Salisbury, Domino, Viceroy and Herbert Tareyton. But no Lucky Strike, Camel or Chesterfield! For

Decade's "let the good times roll," but "Roll your own and save your Roll" was just what Doctor Depression ordered. *Bull Durham* poundage went from 6 million in 1930 to well over 15 million by 1932, enough for more than 3 billion hand-mades. Much of the credit for the resurgence of *Bull Durham* went to George Hill's 35,000 billboards plastered with a John Held, Jr., conception. Its illustration was really a billboard within a billboard. A cow licking her lips stands in a field of clover admiring and "wanting" a *Bull Durham* Bull on a billboard. Above the admiring cow in a cartouche is lettered "Her Hero." The "almost conception" got Hill into a lot of trouble. The poster was removed from the suburbs of San Jose, California, because the church women deemed it an affront to California womanhood. But Hill wasn't deterred by the loss of one billboard, and a later poster had the *Bull* stepping out from behind the fence "to be in clover." *Bull Durham* had a friend in Dashiell Hammett, creator of the "hard-boiled" school of detective fiction. His *The Maltese Falcon*, 1930, featured a chain-smoking, hand-rolling detective by the name of *Sam Spade,* who perversely "rolled-his-own" despite the novel's Twenties setting.

George Washington Hill's answer to the "economy rush" and the overall market loss of 10 billion units was *more* but tamer advertising. His 1931 "Sheep-Dip" campaign for Luckies had caused another furore over advertising ethics and taste. The National Better Business Bureau's criticism fell on deaf ears, but a critical public gave Luckies the "silent" treatment. The ad copy read: " 'TOASTING' expels SHEEP-DIP BASE *naturally* present in *every* tobacco leaf. 'They're *out*—so they can't be in!' ". . . "We sell these expelled irritants to manufacturers of chemical compounds, who use them as a base in making sheep-dip, as well as powerful spraying solution for trees, flowers and shrubs—

some reason "they" could be had at the ball parks. I had been a Giant fan since 1936, but the wartime Giants were going through a "daffiness" era much like the Dodgers of Babe Herman's time. There was still "Master Melvin" pawing the turf in right field waiting another turn at bat, but Johnny Rucker in center, Danny Gardella in left and an infield of Weintraub, Hausman, Jurgess and Sid Gordon, with Lom-

enough to permit the daily dipping of over 50,000 sheep or the daily spraying of many thousands of trees. Thus, you are sure these irritants, naturally present in all tobacco leaves, are not in your LUCKY STRIKE." A squeamish public retreated from Hill's extreme "nature in the raw" thinking. Camel's answer to the downward sales curve, the "ten centers" and Luckies' takeover as No. 1 (1931 statistics: Lucky Strike, 44 billion; Camel, 33 billion units) was to bank its $4,000,000 ad budget for 1932.

Hill and Lasker went back to a more tactful copy board. The stage-and-screen-star testimonial of the late Twenties was revived. The slug line became "Cream of the Crop," but the format remained the same. Jean Harlow said: "I've tried all cigarettes and there's none so good as LUCKIES . . . Put me down as one who always reaches for a LUCKY." Hill took a slap at the new "humidor" cellophane packing without the tab (Camel) when Miss Harlow added: "It's a real delight to find a Cellophane wrapper that opens without an ice pick." Lucky added a brief biography of Harlow and a claim: "SHE'S MISCHIEVOUS, RESTLESS AND 20, WEIGHS 112 POUNDS. Miss Harlow has smoked Luckies for two years . . . not one cent was paid for her signed statement. . . . We appreciate all she writes of Luckies, and so we say, 'Thanks, Jean Harlow.'" A variant on this testimonial was the "O.K. America" theme borrowed from Walter Winchell's "come-on" as gossip columnist on the Lucky Strike Hour, three nights a week over NBC. Hill varied the copy to include "thank yous" to the young women smokers of America: "O.K.—Miss America! We thank you for your patronage." Another ad appealed to Miss America's mother: "I prefer Luckies and so do my daughters." In late 1932 American Tobacco began using color illustrations of women smoking (cigarette in hand), gowned and frocked with a tuxedoed companion in a dream-like

bardi behind the plate, meant anywhere from fifth to eighth place. But we went to see Lombardi hit sky-high, foul home runs, and maybe "be let" steal a base; to see "Ottie" line one, and Gardella get hit on the head with a fly ball; and to watch a marvelously inept relief pitcher named Ken Trinkle, of whom we'd sing a little song: "Twinkle Trinkle, little star...." All this a prelude to the seventh inning "stretch" when

atmosphere that aped the tres snob look of Paramount Pictures' sophisticated comedies. The men were still Arrow collar or Richard Harding Davis types, but the women were now Lombard redheads and Norma Shearer brunettes. The ads and copy (or lack of copy) were thirty years ahead of their time and would influence the pun and visual tie-up of 1960s advertising. A Howard Chandler Christy illustration showed a formally dressed couple having after-dinner coffee on a white tablecloth. The gentleman blows two smoke rings that seem about to circle her fingers. The sole copy line is "forever and ever." The *Lucky Strike* pack appears small on the table and as a larger silhouette on the side of the table cloth. Another ad illustrated a bride holding forth a smoking cigarette. Copy was "I do." The 1931 Pulitzer Prize musical *Of Thee I Sing* was the inspiration for still another "reminder" ad. A cigarette-in-mouth formal young man is serenading his girl (cigarette in hand) with a tenor banjo. Copy is, of course, "Of thee I sing." The *Lucky Strike* pack is again prominent, with the words "It's toasted" barely seen.

The *Journal* of the American Medical Association came across Hill's last "cropper." An angry editorial criticized the 20,679 doctors who answered a *Lucky Strike* questionnaire the *right* way and received free cigarettes. Luckies' copy read: "20,679* Physicians say 'LUCKIES are *less irritating!*'"*"The figures quoted have been checked and certified to by LYBRAND, ROSS BROS. AND MONTGOMERY, Accountants and Auditors." In early '32 Hill put his "nature in the raw" philosophy into a spectacular ad campaign utilizing the finest historical illustrators of the time, and again, copy and visual were coordinated to give a literate and eye-appealing look that made the other brands' ads look about "several minutes out of the trees." Illustrators N. C. Wyeth, Saul Tepper and Harland Frazer painted from history:

we'd rush down to the Cigarette Stand behind the first base mezzanine and, pushing and shoving, line up for the name brands. You were allowed one pack each, but we'd change jackets or coats and go through the line 2 and 3 times. We'd always bring along a nonsmoker or two to stand in line so we'd have extras. If the movie balcony had become our favorite and most convenient "cigarette turf"—3 to 4

Eric the Red, The Fort Dearborn Massacre and The Rape of the Sabines (Lucky copy said "The Raid on the Sabine Women.") The headline running over the violent and often sexy illustrations was: "Nature in the Raw is seldom MILD—and raw tobaccos have no place in cigarettes." After six months the campaign was deemed unsuccessful, even by Hill himself. The "nature in the raw" copy and the violent historical motif were probably too close to the everyday violence of the Bonus Army March and the Harlan County Strike. The wit, "excess" and sophistication of *Lucky Strike's* early Thirties ads bore the stamp of the Twenties. Depression cut-backs had brought in the black-and-white ad, the use of black-and-white photography—notably, the many Edward Steichen campaigns for J.Walter Thompson—and the catalogs of Sears and Montgomery Ward had switched from the expensive, time-consuming line engravings to a greater percentage of the cheaper catalog photography. Hard Times and the "no nonsense" gray of the Thirties replaced a Golden Age of typographic design and color illustration that wouldn't be duplicated until the 1960s. Hill and Lasker, less than content, went back to the simple copy line—depending less on "emotion" and more on "evidence"— and took up the photographic ad for the remainder of the Thirties. Their black-and-white "Center Leaves" demonstration campaign was particularly successful in the 1935–1936 period. Print copy read: "Luckies Use Only the Center Leaves—the Center Leaves Give You the Mildest Smoke." Salesmen would take apart a Lucky and a competing brand and spread the contents on white paper. The *Lucky Strike* gave evidence of less sand and sediment. Hill's compromise still bore a graphic look for this campaign. His photographic ad featured two gentlemen in top hat, white tie and tails, lighting up Luckies. Toward the end of the Thirties, Lucky Strike concentrated on a "professional" testimonial ap-

hours of smoking pleasure without a class "goody-goody" or parent's friends "snitching"—then the most exciting "turf" became the late night "theft" or "borrowing" of someone's family car for moonlit scampers on the parkways and old state roads of Westchester. And if a 50 cent piece and ration stamps were unavailable for a few gallons of replaceable gas, then siphoning of that gas in apartment house

proach. Tobacco auctioneers Jimmy Hicks, Tom Smothers and L. A. "Speed" Riggs gave "witnessed statements" on location in favor of Luckies. The tag line, later to be used effectively on radio with Riggs as the tobacco auctioneer, read: "WITH MEN WHO KNOW TOBACCO BEST—IT'S LUCKIES 2 to 1."

While Hill was being the *enfant terrible* of advertising, *Camel* and *Chesterfield* were plugging away with drab, proven and often repugnant "hard-sell" campaigns. *Camel* came back into print in 1933 with their new moisture-proof cellophane pack. Copy was: "Always kept fresh in the airtight, welded Humidor Pack." "Welded" was hard-sell enough, but the new cellophane packaging wasn't reflected in sales and some price-conscious cigarette manufacturers advertised that "you can't smoke cellophane!" Atypical of *Camel* advertising in the mid-Thirties was the "They Never Get On Your Nerves" campaign. Featuring three to four slug lines reading almost equally well and eight different type faces, *Camels* asked: "ARE YOU A HAIR MUSSER? Those untidy habits come from jangled nerves." Body copy was: ". . . So, if you catch yourself mussing your hair, biting your nails, chewing pencils—or suffering from any other of those countless little nervous habits—Get enough sleep and fresh air—find time for recreation. Make Camels your cigarette. You can smoke as many Camels as you please, for Camels' costlier tobaccos never jangle your nerves." The "For Digestion's SAKE—Smoke Camels" tag was used on a series of testimonial ads ranging from distinguished women of society, such as Mrs. Nicholas Biddle, Philadelphia, and Mrs. Brookfield Van Rensselaer, New York, to the speed boat, rodeo and football heroes of the sports testimonial. *Camels* also ran a series emanating from fine restaurants and hotels, where diners were shown eating different courses in filmclip style, pausing before the entree to "smoke Camels." "Note

garages and on the street could be looked into! We were all about 13 or 14 and Junior Driver's Licences could be had at 16, but only for daytime driving. Our "hot cars" were varied: a 1939 green V-8 Ford; a 1940 gray LaSalle with sliding roof; a 1939 maroon Buick Century with double spares in the front fender wells; and a 1937 black Packard 180 with gearing so adjusted that we could shift from

how they smoothe the way for good digestion." Camel increasingly went after the "woman of action" to go with their already-identified "I'd walk a mile" male and secured testimonials from Aviatrix Jacqueline Cochran and a legion of soon-forgotten local and county female explorers, beekeepers and "ladies of the rapids." Sports-minded Camel turned to the realistic comic strip à la Classic Comics for the brief biography of the rookie "flash" with the dénouement always a shower, a hair comb and a Camel. Headline was: "The Hottest Man on Ice." Copy: "I like my Hockey fast—and my cigarettes slow." Signed, Roy Conacher, Boston Bruins.

While Hill and Lucky Strike were content with the solid "middle-class sending" of Ben Bernie, Mark Warnow, Eddy Duchin and their Orchestras, Camel had the foresight to hire the first of the commercially successful Swing Bands. Benny Goodman's fame had spread from the initial 1935 "Let's Dance" airshots out of the Palomar Ballroom in Los Angeles and the Congress Hotel in Chicago. Hit recordings and a smash success at the Hotel Pennsylvania's Madhattan Room led to a half-hour, prime-time radio show called "The Camel Caravan." Camel gave Goodman sponsor freedom to play what he wanted, and emcees Clifton Fadiman and Robert Benchley and special material by Johnny Mercer made for an exciting show that launched the Swing Era and ingratiated Camels with the new teenage set.

Chesterfield's ad style in the Thirties was mostly good conception but poor execution. A 1931 ad featured a take-off on the current musical hit "The Band Wagon" with Fred and Adele Astaire. The headline was: "Everybody's getting on 'The Band Wagon.'" The illustration of the Astaires was unrecognizable. In 1934 Chesterfield was comparing the aging of wine in casks with their three-year aging of tobacco leaf with the headline:

second to high and back without touching the clutch. Two important props were always brought along: the "love knob" for the steering wheel and the "bean bag" ashtray for our habit. No wonder that last year of the war, 1945, I was sent off to boarding school in the South of Jersey "to get some discipline." My father had "threatened" Culver Military Academy, but I convinced him that "a chalk line"

"It adds something to the Taste and makes them Milder." Gone was "they satisfy," replaced by "the cigarette that's MILDER • the cigarette that TASTES BETTER." *Chesterfield's* famous tag was back the following year. A color photo showed a Sonja Henie–like figure skater rendering "They Satisfy" on ice. If Hill had dealt with the mother-daughter smoking relationship, *Chesterfield* went all the way with a color photograph of a "knitting granny": "Land Sakes! I do believe I'll try one." Copy was getting better and simpler and the single, strong visual (silhouette in color *and* black-and-white) anticipated the Forties look of personalities at Christmas-time playing Santa or themselves with cartons of Chesterfields under their arms and their latest film credits: "Glenn Miller for Chesterfield. Soon to be seen in *Orchestra Wives*." Miller replaced Paul Whiteman on the *Chesterfield* show in December of 1939, and until his entry into the service in 1943 *Chesterfield* had the most popular dance band in the country. Fred Waring and the Pennsylvanians took over for Miller and the "Chesterfield Supper Club" was born, with the old Benny Goodman and Helen Ward vocal hit "Smoke Dreams" *(here by a campfire)* as its theme. Singer Jo Stafford's version with The Starlighters and Paul Weston and his Orchestra became the definitive version and a big hit in 1944.

Old Gold was second to *Lucky Strike* in ad campaign originality. It continued to use a top illustrator (John Held's woodcuts had been particularly successful for them in the Twenties), and the mid-Thirties saw the *Petty Girl* and "Esky" emerge from the pages of *Esquire* magazine to push the "impartial" Public Taste Tests theme of *Old Gold*. "Betty Petty" was always in negligee (red or black), on the phone, or reclining with the phone, sometimes alone and sometimes ruffling the pate of "Esky." Headlines were sexy with much innuendo: "Tortured by a Tele-

could be walked at any one of a dozen eastern Prep Schools. After visiting several, we settled on an ex-Methodist Seminary 8 miles from Princeton, which was renowned for its athletic teams (a 105 to 0 victory over Lawrenceville in 1932 had resulted in severing of athletic relations with the Ivy League Prep Schools) and seemed to be less "sissified" than its better-rated neighbors—Hill, Mercersburg, Blair

phoney?"; "... A Young Man's Fancy Turns"; "Knock, Knock" jokes and puns involving the telephone and *Old Golds.* One campaign was headlined: "Buzzing with news *about Cigarettes!"* Body copy stated: "Yes. Betty Petty is keeping the wires hot. But there's nothing phoney about the new impartial tests of 5 leading brands of *cigarettes* that now *prove* Old Gold A *truly better* Smoke."

In the late Thirties "Swing" had arrived, and cigarette manufacturers hastened to sign up the big Swing Band aggregations for network radio shows. *(Camel* had Benny Goodman; *Chesterfield,* Glenn Miller; Brown & Williamson, Tommy Dorsey for their *Raleigh* and *Kool* brands. Only Hill and *Lucky Strike* stayed with "schmaltz.") In 1938 *Old Gold* hired the most musical of the Big Bands! Artie Shaw was a "teen" sensation with such hits as "Begin the Beguine," "Indian Love Call," "The Carioca," "Rosalie" and the swinging "Back Bay Shuffle." Arrangements by Jerry Gray, the "booting" tenor of Georgie Auld, the drumming of young Buddy Rich and vocals by Helen Forrest and Tony Pastor made Artie Shaw the "King of Clarinet" and later the *"New* King of Swing." But he and *Old Gold* didn't get on too well. Shaw complained that his musical integrity was being compromised by the comedy direction of the series, emceed by Robert Benchley.

The Big Three Standard Brands *and Old Gold* became the Big Five in 1933 with the introduction of *Philip Morris,* an English blend of Philip Morris & Co., Ltd., Inc., now an American firm. An extensive and near-saturation use of radio propelled *Philip Morris* into Standard Brand status and 7 per cent of national cigarette sales by 1940. "Call forrr Phil-lip Mor-eees, Call forrr Phil-lip Mor-eees" *was* the familiar figure and boy soprano sound of Johnny—diminutive John Roventini, an ex-Hotel New Yorker

79

and Peddie. My choice was hastened by an after-lunch visit to the Smoking Area, where it seemed that even the "tykes" (Lower Formers) were indulging. I also had the feeling that it would not be strict and I sensed a rowdy and rebellious aspect about the boys. And a milieu in which I could play the sophisticated New Yorker. What I found for my two years—although a haven from parental strictures—

page—who in calling for *Philip Morris* established a sound as familiar as any in the Golden Age of Radio. Although Standard Brand–priced, *Philip Morris* was identified with the aristocratic and higher priced Turkish blends of the original manufacturer: *English Ovals, Philip Morris Oxford Blues* and *Philip Morris Cambridge.* Johnny and the dramatic fare that his call introduced —*"The Philip Morris Playhouse"*—secured a literate and "class" audience that was attracted by the unusual packaging (the same tobacco-brown as the older English marques) and "personal" selling that Johnny and his silver salver (that had become an American plate) emphasized. Print advertising was negligible as compared to the other Standard Brands. Strip ads showed Johnny head-on or in profile (usually a bust), white-gloved hand to mouth, almost shouting: *"Call for PHILIP MORRIS. America's finest 15¢ Cigarette."* The *Playbill, Vanity Fair, Town & Country* and *Esquire* were the magazines advertised in and "called for."

Brown & Williamson Tobacco of Louisville brought Standard Brand thinking and exploitation to their specialty brands *Raleigh, Kool, Viceroy,* the "roll-your-own" with an enclosed roller, *Target* (50 smokes for 10¢), and "ten centers" *Wings* and *Avalon.* Originally a small snuff firm out of Winston-Salem, B & W was purchased by the British-American Tobacco Company in 1927 and brought out the first *Camel*-copied *Raleigh* in 1929 for 20¢. A revival of coupons and premiums went with the repackaged and Depression-priced *Raleigh, Kool* (derived from the earlier mentholated *Spud*) and 1936 filter-tipped *Viceroy. Kool* was heavily advertised via Willie the Penguin and Tommy Dorsey and his Orchestra in the late Thirties.

The late Twenties and the early days of the Depression saw a proliferation of small-volume brands: regional, experimental, mentholated, city and county-wide brands with door-to-door

Studs Lonigan, on the verge of fifteen, and wearing his first suit of long trousers, stood in the bathroom with a SWEET CAPORAL pasted in his mug... He puffed, drew the fag out of his mouth, inhaled and said to himself: Well, I'm kissing the old dump goodbye tonight.

—James T. Farrell,
YOUNG LONIGAN, 1932

(Top) Dime novel "virtue" and Frank Merriwell are forgotten as a high school debating team primps "tough" with unlit cigarettes and (silhouette) turn-of-the-century street urchins "mug" knowingly for the camera. But (bottom, left) by the Forties—after scores of Warner Brothers gangster films—this Hell's Kitchen pair *could* be taken at "face" value.

Mother : 'AUGUSTUS, YOU NAUGHTY BOY, YOU'VE BEE
SMOKING. DO YOU FEEL VERY BAD, DEAR ?'
Augustus : THANK YOU—I'M ONLY DYING.'

A step before long pants—and easier to obtain—first smokes varied with
locale: farm youth smoked cornsilk and Booth Tarkington's *Penrod* hid hay-
seed cigarettes; city youth could purchase *Cubebs*—"no tobacco or habit
forming drugs"—at any drugstore, 12 for 5¢. And upon cigarette manhood—
"Sweet Caps" (*Sweet Caporal*) or *Piedmont*, 20 for 5¢.

C IGARETTE *was making
scorn of her doom of Sex,
dancing it down, drinking it
down, laughing it down, burning it out in tobacco fumes,
drowning it in trembling cas-
cades of wine, trampling it to
dust under the can-can by
her little brass-bound boots,
till there was scarce a trace
of it left in this prettiest
and wildest little scamp of
all the Army of Africa.*

—Ouida,
UNDER TWO FLAGS, 1896

Ladies of the evening all! In the theatre or "on the streets," women who
smoked in public were condemned by the bourgeois society of nineteenth-
century Europe. (Top, right) English actress Lily Langtry, on an 1887 U.S. tour,
was the first woman to be photographed smoking. (Above) A "ragazza marina,"
off the streets of Napoli, assumes an apache-like pose.

(Clockwise) Miss Sylvia Grey of London does a cupid's bow exhale, while in Boston a lion tamer's assistant accepts a cigarette prop. (Above) Aging Lola Montez—actress, courtesan and "great female Republican"—informed New York Herald reporters that she smoked 500 cigarettes a day! One reporter wryly observed that smoking had made "inroads on her beauty."

SHE LEFT
HOME UNDER
A CLOUD

The middle Twenties saw millions of women smoking, and (clockwise) some-body's bob-haired daughter lighting up a maiden aunt; John Held flappers forever going somewhere in "a cloud of smoke"; and cigarette extension holders wafted in sexual insouciance. Even Michael Arlen's *The Green Hat* could boast of a heroine, Iris Storm, who "coughed the cigarette cough."

Saville Row–tailored Adolphe Menjou neatly bisects his waxed moustache
with the perfect light! From Hecht-MacArthur's *Front Page* in 1931 to Stanley
Kubrick's *Paths of Glory* in 1958, Menjou smoked his sartorial way from "top
hat" to "top brass." (Inset) Hero or villain, Brian Donlevy also wore clothes
and cigarettes well. Here, as *Alias Heliotrope Harry*.

To paraphrase George Sand—the man was nothing, the cigarette everything! (Clockwise) Pre–*Thin Man* William Powell in a 1927 silent, *Love's Greatest Mistake;* Fred Astaire as World War I dancer-ace, Vernon Castle; Noel Coward as Noel Coward, 1933; and John Barrymore, straight-on, in a 1938 Fox turkey— *Hold That Coed!*

Erich von Stroheim—out of uniform, monocle, perfume, dressing gown and pistol range! But not out of cigarettes! Here, chain-lighting a Turkish "bomber." Né Erich Oswald Stroheim of Prussian-Jewish background, von Stroheim capitalized on the "dirty Hun" sentiment of WWI with such villainous roles as Lt. von Steuben in *Blind Husbands* and Count Karamzin in *Foolish Wives.*

(Clockwise) Stroheim as Lt. Erich von Steuben, *Blind Husbands*, 1918; a Twenties publicity still used by Paramount for Billy Wilder's 1943 *Five Graves to Cairo* with Stroheim as Field Marshal Rommel; Jean Renoir's *La Grande Illusion*, 1937, with Stroheim playing the sympathetic Commander von Rauffenstein; and as Count Vladislav Sergei Karamzin in *Foolish Wives*, 1921.

These men would offer you a cigarette—your last—for certain information: (Clockwise) Anthony Quinn as a sadistic war lord in *China Sky*, 1943; Peter Lorre, in his first role as a Nazi, *The Cross of Lorraine*, 1943; Brian Donlevy as the evil Lejaune in *Beau Geste*, 1939; and Hume Cronyn as Captain Munsey in *Brute Force*, 1947.

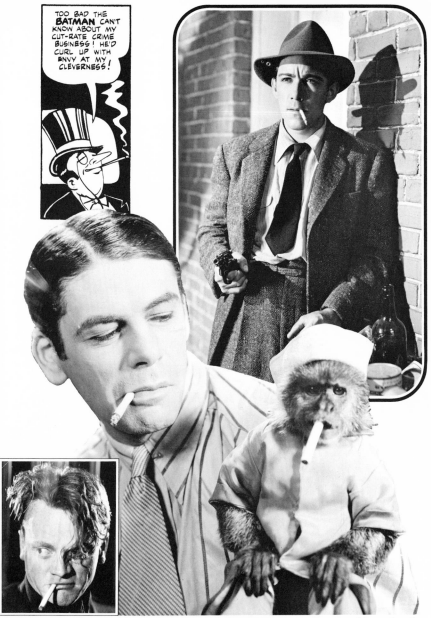

These men made no offers! They kept their cigarettes and everything else for themselves: (Clockwise) Anthony Quinn, in the alley and dangerous, *Parole Fixer*, 1938; Paul Muni, with *friend*, as "*Scarface*" Camonte in Howard Hawks' *Scarface: The Shame of a Nation*, 1932; and James Cagney in Warner Brothers' first gangster hit, *The Public Enemy*, 1931.

Spade, barefooted in green and white checked pajamas, sat on the side of his bed. He scowled at the telephone on the table while his hands took from beside it a packet of brown papers and a sack of BULL DURHAM... Spade's thick fingers made a cigarette with deliberate care, sifting a measured quantity of tan flakes down into curved paper, spreading the flakes so that they lay equal at the ends with a slight depression in the middle, thumbs rolling the paper's inner edge down and up under the outer edge as forefingers pressed it over, thumbs and fingers sliding to the paper cylinder's ends to hold it even while the tongue licked the flap, left forefinger and thumb pinching their end while right forefinger and thumb smoothed the damp seam, right forefinger and thumb twisted their end and lifting the other to Spade's mouth.

—Dashiel Hammett,
THE MALTESE FALCON, 1929

"By Gad, sir, you *are* a character!"—Caspar Gutman (Sydney Greenstreet) to Sam Spade (Humphrey Bogart) in John Huston's *The Maltese Falcon*, 1941. Humphrey De Forest Bogart—high-waisted, slouch-hatted, trench-coated and very nicotined—*was* the cynical, acid-tongued, laconic Private Eye/Existentialist Hero out of the pages of Dashiell Hammett and Raymond Chandler.

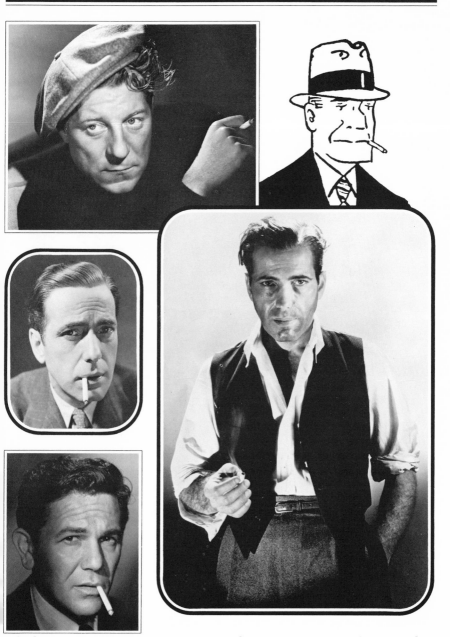

(Clockwise) A roach of a *Gitanes* or *Gauloises* hanging from the lower lip, Jean Gabin was to pre-war France what Bogart was to the Forties; Chester Gould's *Dick Tracy*, a heavy smoker in the early years of the strip; Bogie again, in Archie Mayo's *Black Legion*, 1937; and the Lower East Side Bogart—"street boy" John Garfield in Abe Polonsky's *Force of Evil*, 1948.

The mien of the man in the street: (Clockwise) James Gleason—big-city, small-time and honest; Lon Chaney—"man of a thousand faces," but the *one* to have on your side; Victor McLaglen—big and bumbling with a heart of gold—here, in the Fox film, *Rackety Rax;* and Phil Regan, Warner Brothers' golden tenor of the Irish Ghetto, 1935.

The mien of the man in Woman's Clubs' hearts: (Clockwise) Charles Boyer as the romantic sculptor who woos Irene Dunne in *Together Again;* outdoorsman and indoorsman—pre-moustached Clark Gable, 1932; and Rudolph Valentino—in his last and best film, *Son of the Sheik,* 1926—who always seemed to be doing the things that kept everybody's mind on Sex.

Cass waited in front, watching an Irish boy and an Italian playing rotation, and wishing that he had fifteen cents for a pack of CAMELS. He was tired of rolling his own all the time, a nickel a sack, like some hick from the country.

—Nelson Algren,
SOMEBODY IN BOOTS, 1935

GENUINE
DURHAM
(Trade Mark)

SMOKING TOBACCO.
Manufactured by
W.T. BLACKWELL & CO.,
(BLACKWELL'S DURHAM TOB. CO. Suc'r.)
DURHAM, N. C.
THE AMERICAN TOBACCO CO., SUCCESSOR

"Roll your own" *Bull Durham* accounted for 14 billion "hand-mades" in 1914, more than all ready-made smokes combined. A nickel sack meant 33 cigarettes in the hands of a skilled roller. (Clockwise) Tom Mix whirls and "rolls" while Cagney "seals one" in *The Oklahoma Kid*, 1939. And kindly Jean Hersholt demonstrates that the "makin's" aren't just for tough guys.

Marlene Dietrich was the female nonpareil in the cinematic pantheon of smokers. She had a head start—coming from the decadent, amoral and narcissistic Germany of the Twenties—but it was through her Svengali, Director Josef von Sternberg, that she dragged her cigarette beauty around with her the way an errant Rothschild might forever drive a dented-fender Bentley.

(Top, left) "See What the Boys in the Backroom Will Have"—and what they had, *sans* von Sternberg, was a Marlene Dietrich that was bawdy and hard-boiled, a "Claire Trevor with legs" in *Destry Rides Again*, 1939; and (silhouette) the object, no less, of two high-wire linemen, Edward G. Robinson and George Raft, in Raoul Walsh's *Manpower*, 1941.

In the Hollywood of the Thirties and Forties, bad girls had the "blues" and bad girls had "cigarettes." (Clockwise) Virginia Mayo on a barstool in *She's Working Her Way Through College;* Alice Faye and a "Fanny Brice" lamppost *In Old Chicago,* 1938; and Greta Garbo in the all-talking, all-smoking 1930 screen version of Eugene O'Neill's stage success, *Anna Christie.*

(Clockwise) "Blues——from my head to my shoes, I'm blue today!" Joe Oliver's 1928 classic, *West End Blues;* Dime-A-Dance line-up—Eve Arden, second from left, and Marlene Dietrich, center, in *Manpower*, 1941; Lana Turner getting a light in *Johnny Eager*, 1941; Rita Hayworth luxuriating in *Gilda*, 1946; and Lauren Bacall in Howard Hawks' *The Big Sleep*, 1946.

Man, they say he's an old junkie, he's old and funky, all that . . . that's not nice. Whatever they do, let them do that and enjoy themselves, and you get your kicks yourself. All I do is smoke some New Orleans cigarettes, don't sniff nothing in my nose, nothing. I drink and I smoke and that's all . . . My business is the musical thing, all the way . . .

—Lester Young,
   Paris, 1958

Lester Young "lighting up" in photographer Gjon Mili's *Jammin' the Blues*, 1944. Precursor of the "sound" in Modern Jazz; creator of phraseology (both played and spoken); originator of, and model for, the Hipster of the Forties— "Prez" smoked and played his "you can't catch me" music in out-sized pin-stripes, pork-pie hat, suede shoes, and Benzedrine-soaked gum.

One man's opinion! On the wagon in 1936, W. C. Fields tried cigarettes with little success but regaled friends with the above practice. A few years later, Fields quit Lucky Strike as a sponsor, and smoking forever, in protest over cigarette commercials. (Inset) Harpo Marx showed a good "bite" in *The Cocoanuts*, 1925.

A cigarette that bears a teardrop's traces! (Clockwise) Lloyd Hamilton in Fox's *Show of Shows*, 1929; W. C. Fields at his Toluca Lake residence with cigarette and without his daily ration of martinis; Harry Langdon in *The Hitchhiker*, 1932. And Harpo Marx—madder than sadder—in Paramount's *Animal Crackers*, 1930.

Bond took out his black gunmetal cigarette-box and his black-oxidized Ronson lighter and put them on the desk beside him. He lit a cigarette, one of the Macedonian blend with the three gold rings round the butt that Morlands of Grosvenor Street made for him, then he settled himself forward in the padded swivel chair and began to read.

—Ian Fleming,
MOONRAKER, 1955

(Clockwise) Edward R. Murrow's commitment, revealed through countless pursed and hapless cigarettes, made his CBS *See It Now* programs among the most literate and courageous of television's Golden Age; FDR's switch from pipe to cigarette and holder greatly influenced cigarette sales in the Thirties and Forties; and Ian Fleming extolled that "first delicious cigarette."

(Clockwise) *Allen and Ginter* of Richmond, one of the top four cigarette firms in 1880, a year in which 409,000,000 "hand-mades" were sold; a 1915 *Murad* illustration with a visual scope worthy of the Pharaohs; and an 1885 ad— "Dr. Scott's electric cigarettes. No matches required. They light on the box. A wad of absorbent cotton in the mouthpiece strains the nicotine."

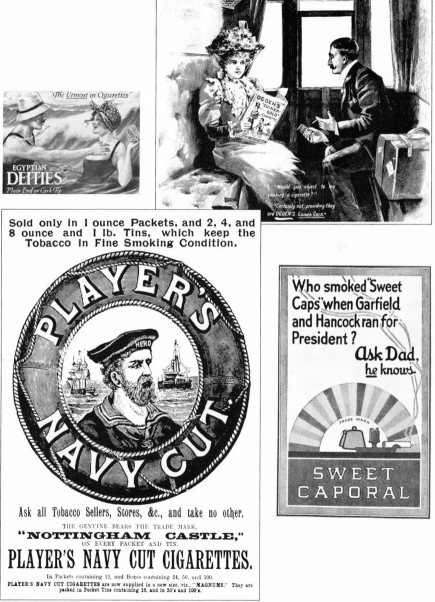

(Clockwise) Heyday of the Gibson Girl "bathing costume" and the all-Turkish smoke—American Tobacco's *Egyptian Deities,* 1905; young American Tobacco scion George Hill's first ad campaign—"Ask Dad, he knows"—for *Sweet Caporal,* 1916; and original *Player's* Navy Cut Cigarettes—"in packets containing 12, and boxes of 24, 50 and 100."

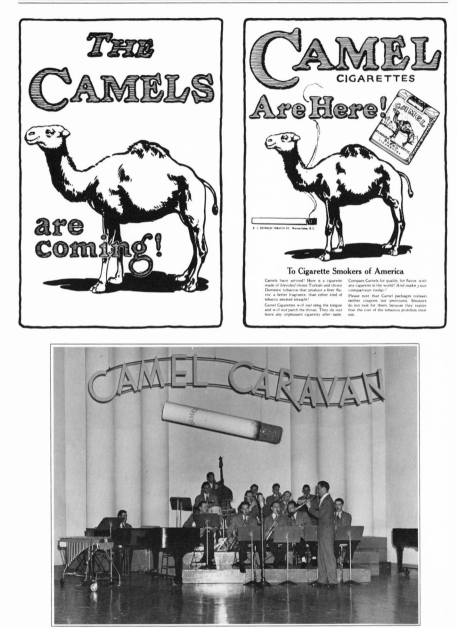

(Clockwise) R. J. Reynolds launched *Camels* in 1914 with the then unheard-of ad budget of $1,500,000 and ushered in the era of the "standard brands." Adapted from *Prince Albert* smoking tobacco, "The Hump" was so successful that by 1918 straight Turkish and straight domestic smokes were "back in the pack." Big Bands meant Big Sales in the Thirties! Here, Benny Goodman on the *Camel Hour*.

(Clockwise) A middle-Thirties Art Deco ad for the all-Turkish *Ramases. Spud,* the first mentholated cigarette, was the invention of Lloyd "Spud" Hughes of Mingo Junction, Ohio, who found a way to impregnate tobacco with menthol. He later sold out to Axton-Fisher Tobacco, and *Spud* became one of the big sellers of the Thirties. A John Held, Jr., "silent movie" illustration campaign for *Old Gold,* 1928.

"Calllll forrr Phil-lip Mor-eees!" The familiar figure and boy soprano sound of Johnny—diminutive John Roventini—calling for Philip Morris became one of the most penetrating images on radio in the Thirties and Forties. With the clop-clop music of Ferde Grofé as background, Johnny presented *The Philip Morris Playhouse*—dramatic fare starring Dietrich, Meredith, Barrymore, et al.

George Washington Hill *could* tell a lie ... an ad lie ... just a fib, no bigger than a cigarette ... and as he told many fibs he sold many cigarettes. Prexy of American Tobacco, 1925-1946, Hill was the greatest ad genius of his time, and campaigns such as "Reach for a *Lucky* Instead of a Sweet," "Lucky Strike Green Has Gone to War" and "L.S./M.F.T." rank near the top in "ad-dom."

"Just gimme th' aspirin. I already got a Purple Heart."

(Top) The biggest ad story and finest ad campaign of the Forties—"Lucky Strike Green Has Gone to War"—produced an incredible 38% sales rise in 1942. The elimination of the solid green (chromium base) on Lucky packages provided enough bronze for 400 light tanks. Most of the new Lucky packs ended up with Bill Mauldin's "Dogface" of World War II cartoon fame.

*was a double standard between student and athlete. God help you
if you were neither student nor athlete! But I was part student, part
athlete and all Bugler! For $150.00 per year I was hired as School
Bugler (my application had stated trumpet for band and orchestra)
which made me privy to the school grounds most all hours. I was the
only one up and about legally after Taps and before Reveille and took*

selling. Brand names were "down-home" and "tacky" as a half-
century before, while packaging was as graphically lurid as
Street & Smith's dime pulps. Brands had no advertising (except
maybe an ad in a local paper), and the tobaccos, more than likely,
were "savin's" instead of "makin's." *Spud* cigarettes bore the
very personal stamp of Lloyd "Spud" Hughes. Out of Mingo
Junction, Ohio, Hughes, a backyard speed enthusiast and front-
line eccentric, had invented a way to impregnate tobacco with
menthol in the early Twenties. Traveling by car, literally door-
to-door, Hughes built up a "personalized" following for his
signatured cigarette in the bottom lands of Ohio and Kentucky.
In 1926 Axton-Fisher of nearby Louisville offered Hughes
$90,000 for his *Spud* cigarette. Hughes thought a moment, took
the money and went off in a $90,000 burst of speed for the rest
of the Twenties. He survived racing car and plane crack-ups
only to succumb to the bigger Crash! *Spud,* the cigarette, went
on to become the fifth-largest-selling cigarette of the Thirties.
Heavy advertising was directed at the "smart set" of polo ponies,
Caribbean cruises and night clubs illustrated in a watercolor
wash style.

If *Spud* and "Spud" Hughes were a Horatio Alger story and
an Alger story in reverse, the majority of the "down-home"
regionals were either "ekin's" for the small manufacturer or
ethnic and rural "favors" by the larger companies.

Axton-Fisher Tobacco of Louisville and St. Louis had: *Clown,
Thrills* and *Skeet.* Rosedor Cigarette Company: Menthorets
(Mentholated Cigarettes. "Pleases As It Eases") and *Bright Star.*
Continental Tobacco Company (subsidiary of Philip Morris) had:
Barking Dog and *Cigarette Time* (mentholated); Scotten, Dillon
Company, Detroit, had: *Yankee Girl* and *Ramrod;* Liggett &
Myers had: *Picayune* ("Pride of New Orleans") and *Old Mill*

113

*those occasions for sampling my new cigarette brand. I had given up
the illuminated letter of the Chesterfield package for the more daring,
warning bull's-eye of Lucky Strike. Looking back, my job as Bugler
could be likened to a "trusty" in a reformatory or prison. I often went
to town after Taps to secure cigarettes, candy, malts, etc. for the boys
in my hall. Every boarding school has a designated area where smok-*

("Old Belt Tobacco"); Reed Tobacco, branch of Larus Brothers,
had: *Domino, Airline;* R. R. Tobin Tobacco: *Cookie Jar;* The
Health Cigar Company, N.Y.: *Sano* (1% nicotine); Lincoln &
Ulmer, N.Y.: *O-NIC-O* (less than 1% nicotine); Ko Wah Lum,
San Francisco: *Fook Look Cigarettes;* American Tobacco Company: *111* (1 part Turkish, 1 part Virginia, 1 part Burley: 24 cigarettes for 15¢); The Winston Tobacco Company: *Fems* ("Crim-
son tips for the lips"), Hed Kleer Tobacco Company: *Hed Kleer*
("The Original Eucalyptus Smoke"); Fleming-Hall Tobacco:
Skis (mentholated); Paul A. Werner, N.Y.: *Snowball* (menthol
treated); and Alliance Cigar Company: *Puppies.*

The Last Holdout to the all-consuming popularity of the cigarette was the Cigarette Girl herself! In Twenties speakeasies
she chanted a tobacco immemorial: "Cigars, Cigarettes!" The
Ziegfeld Follies of 1931 changed all that with Mack Gordon and
Harry Revel's tune "Cigarettes, Cigars!" An on-stage recitation
went: "Chesterfields, Camels, Luckies, cigars! I peddle my wares
to 'coked' millionaires, Rough guys and hoboes, street girls with
no beaux—Penniless phonies who figure the ponies and try to
be men of affairs."

Hollywood in the Thirties peddled its cigarette "awares" with
snap-brim authority, low-key lighting and Warner Brothers'
"butcher-boy" cost-cutting. *Sound,* and its fury, smashed the
mannered, uneasy extension-holder stance of the Twenties, and
"smoking permitted in the balcony" became the smoking "seen"
on the silver screen! Lives were programmed reel-by-reel and
cigarette-by-cigarette. Paul Muni in Mervyn LeRoy's *I Am a
Fugitive from a Chain Gang* becomes the "social-injustice"
smoker. Shivering cold and harassed, he replies to his sweetheart's: "But how do you get along; how do you live?" with the
choked animal reply, "I steal." Josef von Sternberg's *Shanghai*

ing is permitted and "masters" aren't—somewhat like a reverse "offi-cers' country." Ours was a small Victorian house directly across from the main building, dubbed "The Colonel," where amid pool tables, much smoke and hidden booze, ruled The Phoenixville Boys—Pennsyl-vania's coal-and-anthracite answer to Hollywood's Bowery Boys and Dead End Kids. They were the conscripted athletes (most were Marine

Express utilizes a billowing lungful to obscure the inviolate nar-cissism of Marlene Dietrich. Herbert Marshall, in Ernst Lub-itsch's *Trouble in Paradise*, plays an unrepentant jewel thief and holds a cigarette and smokes as if his cigarette holding arm were broken. The cigarette portrays the beginnings of the Depression's "shirtsleeves-to-shirtsleeves" mobility in Mervyn LeRoy's *Three On a Match*. Three former school friends (Bette Davis, Joan Blondell and Ann Dvorak) meet years later for a reunion and light their cigarettes from the same match—then remember the superstition of bad luck. Ann Dvorak, as the socialite, falls on Depression days and dies in gangster degradation. The surviving Joan Blondell and Bette Davis take a light from another match and flippantly throw it away.

Films of the Thirties set up smoking in ethnic and psycholog-ical categories: Humphrey Bogart, Spencer Tracy and Jimmy Cagney (even when not smoking, but playing end-over-end with a cigarette in *The Crowd Roars*) were "Machismo" smokers. Fred Astaire and Clifton Webb were "Light-on-their-Effete" smokers. Franchot Tone and Henry Fonda were "Poor-Little-Rich-Boy" smokers. Peter Lorre and Edward G. Robinson were "Levantine" smokers. And Joan Blondell, Bette Davis and Ann Dvorak were "Street-Girl" smokers.

From childhood of the First Cigarette Generation to the youth of the Standard Brands Generation seemed like eternity; the youth of the Standard Brands Generation to the manhood of the Last Cigarette Generation was a season. World War II, and its aftermath, would bring age in a night to the Last Cigarette Generation.

FIRST JOE: Got a butt?
SECOND JOE: Mmmmmm.
FIRST JOE: How 'bout a light?
SECOND JOE: Mmmmmm. How're you fixed for spit!

—G.I. Conversation,
  WORLD WAR II

hen James Jones's *From Here to Eternity* hero, Regular Army Private Robert E. Lee Prewitt, "lit a tailormade" at Schofield Barracks, Oahu, just before Pearl Harbor, a rural, masculine, straight Bright tobacco era came to an end forever! The Depression revival of "roll-your-own" *Bull Durham* and *Target,* the "economy brands" and the "regionals" passed into Cigarette History. They would have a brief fling during World War II rationing (when every available tobacco scrap was packaged and sold), but as the days of peace ran out, urbanization, war production and a new term—"modern design"—insured that the beginnings of a newer, even more competitive cigarette industry were in the "makin's."

The new "makin's" had its basis in modern design. Bauhaus derived! The teardrop automobile shape; the functional, unadorned building look; the streamlined *Burlington Zephyr;* and the shark-nosed Curtiss P-40 all came to a head at the New York World's Fair in 1939. Even the classic Lucky Strike Green package was cleaned up! Toward the end of the Fair, Raymond Loewy redesigned the pack by repeating the bull's-eye front and back and turned the proportion lettering of the word "cigarettes" into a simple, legible gothic. And President Franklin D. Roosevelt, a pipe smoker since the Twenties, switched to a long cigarette and holder, setting the stage for *Pall Mall's* prewar declaration that "Something is happening in the cigarette business!" "Modern design" in smoking meant the king-sized cigarette, and king-size meant that "in Pall Mall the additional length travels the smoke further—giving you not alone a longer cigarette but a better cigarette—a definitely milder, a definitely cooler smoke." *Pall Mall* had been around for years as an American Tobacco subsidiary product, an expensive, straight Turkish smoke, boxed in a dozen different shapes and sizes. But in 1936

vets) *taking senior year over to get college football scholarships. Our quarterback's brother had been the Philadelphia Eagles prewar quarterback, and our halfback's brother had broken Eric Tipton's college punting record while at Georgia and was then "booming them" for the Pitt Steelers. Our line averaged over 200 pounds, and a completely victorious season was capped by a 27-6 rout of the Doug*

the Turkish flavor was dropped for a Bright blend and the packaging and price went regular to compete with the standard brands. Then, in 1939, "modern design." *Pall Mall* was given a "modern blend"—a Burley mixture like the standard brands— the standard length of 70 millimeters was kinged to 85 millimeters, and sales doubled within the year. American Tobacco also kinged *Herbert Tareyton,* retaining its cork tip.

The king-sized cigarette wasn't new—Brown & Williamson had its *Viceroy* king with filter as far back as 1936, and Rum & Maple had borrowed cartoonist Otto Soglow's "Little King" for its *Little King* 85 millimeter in 1940. But American Tobacco's advertising strength via radio, print and packaging changed the course of the cigarette industry. *Pall Mall's* print campaign copy identified "modern design" (its new length) with rearmament in guns, tanks and planes, while incessant radio spots—close to 5,000 times a week—chanted "On the land, in the air and on the sea" cued by the rising beep, beep, beep of a destroyer whistle. By 1951 each of the Big Six manufacturers had a king-sized brand alongside its regular, and by 1953 "kings" accounted for twenty-five per cent of the U.S. market. In 1956 each manufacturer was promoting a regular, a king and two filter brands!

Where there's war there's smoke. Cigarette smoke! From Acre to Balaclava, Khartoum, Pretoria, Vimy Ridge and the Battle of the Bulge, war changed cigarette and smoking habits. Lucky Strike Green went to war in 1942. George Washington Hill's most famous campaign—"Lucky Strike Green Has Gone to War"— broke about the time of the Allied invasion of Casablanca and Oran, and in a few months *Lucky Strike* sales increased almost forty per cent. Yet, in the whole prior decade, 1930–1940, Lucky sales had remained about where they started. With the increasing war effort and urbanization, cigarette consumption zoomed.

Kenna-led Army Plebes. In most respects my boarding school days were a non-military academy version of Calder Willingham's novel "End As A Man." We had: an athlete-run "protection racket"; the old prep-school fear of saltpeter in the food; a goodly selection of Latin students who were fined a dime for every Spanish word said at dinner table but allowed to speak Spanish at all other times; the boyish

Nineteen-forty cigarette production was 189,371,258,000. In 1947 it was 369,682,768,000. Almost double. Eighteen per cent of the cigarette output during the period 1941–1945, or 222.6 billion cigarettes, were sent overseas. "Shorts" on the home front created an insatiable demand for cigarettes. Long lines of customers queued up at tobacco shops for the standard brands, but often came away with a pack of *Coffee-Tone, Fleetwood, Fatima,* or, at best, a *Raleigh* or *Viceroy!*

The G.I.s overseas had no such problem! As in past wars, commanders, like Pershing and then MacArthur, called for cigarettes and got them! To supplement his pay in foreign money, the G.I. took to using his "deck of butts" or cartons to buy merchandise on the black market. The bartered cigarettes soon became the only stable currency in war-ravaged Europe and remained so for two years after V-E Day.

Print advertising was still a potent sales force in the Forties, and George Washington Hill, ad head and president of American Tobacco, once again dominated the cigarette advertising industry with his good taste, brilliant copy and clean-looking ads. In 1942 Hill commissioned well-known artists to "paint from life" in the tobacco country. Boxed illustrations by James Chapin, Thomas Hart Benton and a young David Stone Martin were headlined: *"Lucky Strike* Means Fine Tobacco." Those five words became so well known through print and radio that by 1944 "L.S./M.F.T." appeared on the bottom of every *Lucky Strike* pack. Other Hill campaigns featured tobacco auctioneers photographed on location in the warehouse, and one auctioneer —L. A. "Speed" Riggs—went on to radio fame as the auctioneering voice of "Sold American" on the Lucky Strike Hit Parade.

George W. Hill's competition stressed "identity" through testimonials, a reliance on the snob value of chic locales, and *thespian complete with cloak and ham voice; the young entrepreneurs who sold ham-and-cheese sandwiches at a dime apiece; and the "Coke-bottle smokes" (the burning cigarette was held face down into the bottle until time for another exhale out the window). An era best summed up by an escape from the Sunday Night Dinner—"Tuni-noodle"—to the Highway Diner of hamburgers, french-fries and cig-*

an unabashed display of the World War II fighting man. *Chester-field* had: 1942—"Keep 'em Smokin'—Our fighting men rate the best" (color photo of G.I. in battle dress); a service testimonial with Joan Bennett (color photo) in an American Women's Voluntary Services Uniform saying—"His cigarette and mine"; the straight testimonial with Rise Stevens as the Metropolitan Opera's world-famous *Carmen*—"You might say I'm careful"; and in 1946—"The Largest Selling Cigarette at Sherman Billingsley's Stork Club" (color photo of Stork Club cigarette girl.) *Camel,* off-again, on-again No. 1, was more blunt: 1941—"5 extra smokes per pack by burning 25% slower than the average of the 4 other largest selling brands tested"; 1942—"Camels are the favorite! in the army . . . in the navy . . . in the marine corps . . . in the coast guard"; also 1942—"You want steady nerves when you're flying Uncle Sam's bombers across the ocean. (Names withheld for defense purposes and national security"). And *Old Gold* had: "Why be irritated? Light an Old Gold," and in 1945 something that went: "Apple Honey helps guard O.Gs from cigarette dryness."

If Hill's work was several cuts above the competition in print, then in radio, at his worst, it was several decibels! He had been drumming the radio beat since 1928, when his "Reach for a *Lucky* Instead of a Sweet" was featured on the Lucky Strike Radio Hour. By 1930 Luckies had passed *Camels* and were No. 1 in sales, and Hill had become one of radio's biggest spenders. In the Thirties he used the Metropolitan Opera, the Hit Parade, Ben Bernie and All the Lads, Eddie Duchin, Jack Benny, Phil Harris, Wayne King and even a reluctant W. C. Fields. Fields, like Henry Morgan in the Forties, made the tobacco hawkers his special target and quit *Lucky Strike* and smoking forever in protest over their print and radio commercials. During the war years Hill

arettes, all programmed by the "juke" of Ted Weems' "Heartaches," Louis Armstrong's "The Gypsy" and Lionel Hampton's "Hey-Ba-Ba-Re-Bop." Cigarette Manhood was reached on entering college. No more Sen-Sen, hot-showered bathrooms after a smoke, replacement of awful Virginia Rounds and Herbert Tareytons from my mother's cache of "guests smokes," or any of the 101 furtive and exciting things that

saturated radio with "Lucky Strike Green Has Gone to War," "L.S./M.F.T." and "Sold American" on Information Please, Kay Kyser's College of Musical Knowledge and the Lucky Strike Hit Parade.

If Hill had a taste lapse, it was in the field of popular music. He demanded "absolute melody" and got it from the succession of Sweet Bands that he hired for their "Mickey Mouse" touch: Eddy Duchin, Ben Bernie, Kay Kyser and the Mark Warnow orchestra of "Your Hit Parade" played the hits so that Luckies' already-won middle-class audience would stay tuned for the commercials. In the vocal area Hill was more adamant. He liked and hired: belting-on-the-beat Sophie Tucker; the girl-next-door vocalizing of Ginny Sims on Kay Kyser's College of Musical Knowledge; the coy, "bo-peep" style of "Wee" Bonnie Baker; and the stand-up, "stout-hearted" style of Hit Parade vocalists Barry Wood, Lanny Ross and operatic tenor Lawrence Tibbett. He disliked Frank Sinatra (his 1943 Hit Parade vocalist) for his lazy, "swooning" style, and the following season saw Lawrence Tibbett "booming" the top ten hits. All this conservative taste meant that, from the middle Thirties on, *Lucky Strike* had no youth market show on radio. Swing Music was Youth Music, and Benny Goodman for *Camel*, Glenn Miller for *Chesterfield* and Tommy Dorsey for *Kool* and *Raleigh* were to take away considerable first and young cigarette sales from *Lucky Strike*.

In 1946, the year of Hill's death, Frederic Wakeman published *The Hucksters*, a satiric novel of then radio-dominated Madison Avenue. And George Washington Hill sat for some or part of a brutal portrait. The product was soap, not cigarettes. Beautee Soap. And the sadistic chairman of the board was called Evan Llewelyn Evans. Victor Norman was the cynical, tough, "creative" account executive—the "huckster" of Radio City. Evans

*made smoking a youthful adventure. Smoking had become a habit—
and legal! And then, suddenly, in my senior year, First Quits! I had
been an excessive smoker for 8 years, but I decided to quit—"just like
that!" Was this Joseph Conrad's Shadow Line—"a warning that the
region of early youth must be left behind"? Or was it a return to some
Horatio Alger resolve we had made for ourselves, but had long for-*

was portrayed as a "rugged individualist" impresario. A Ziegfeld with soap! Complete with funny hats (always worn indoors)
and a fondness for expectorating on the boardroom table to
make a point. The best-seller went to Hollywood and came back
with Clark Gable as Victor Norman and Sydney Greenstreet as
Evan Llewelyn Evans. Greenstreet had a field day with the part
and Gable was still King, but most of Hill's ads—some of them
after forty years—read better than Mr. Wakeman's book.

Humphrey De Forest Bogart and William H. "Bill" Mauldin
were the best friends and salesmen the cigarette industry had
during World War II. All the radio spots, print slogans, tobacco
auctioneers, packaged and repackaged designs, hero and heroine
testimonials were just "reminder floss" compared to *their* effect
on the Last Cigarette Generation!

"Bogart is a man with a past," wrote French critic André
Bazin. "When he comes into a film it is already 'the morning
after'; his face scarred by what he has seen, and his step heavy
from all that he has learned, having ten times triumphed over
death, he will surely survive for us one more time."

Bogart survived being "The Real Maud Humphrey Baby" (his
mother was noted magazine illustrator Maud Humphrey; his
father, Belmont Bogart, a New York society physician) and went
on to become Roy Earle, Sam Spade, Rick Leland, Rick, Sgt. Joe
Gunn, Matrac, Harry Morgan, Philip Marlowe and Dobbs. In his
survival kit were *Chesterfields*. But in his hands they weren't
just cigarettes. They were deployed as tools of bitterness and
amusement at a world seething with duplicity. Bogart doesn't
just exhale! As Philip Marlowe in Raymond Chandler's *The Big
Sleep*: "I lit the cigarette and blew a lungful at him and he sniffed
it like a terrier at a rathole." As Sam Spade in Dashiell Hammett's
The Maltese Falcon: "Spade put the cigarette in his mouth, set

gotten? It turned out to be only a consolidation of our energies, a gird for some forthcoming (hoped for) great event. Second Quits was also —"just like that!"—on returning to New York after a G.I. Bill sampling of the fleshpots of Europe and an addiction to Gauloises cigarettes. Third Quits doesn't count! It was a "Hundred Dollar Understanding." A bet undertaken for a week and paid off in pennies, and rightly so!

fire to it, and laughed smoke out." Ultimately, if with Bogart a "drag" was a moral commitment, then an "exhale" was an "I won't play the sap for *you*."

In broader terms, Hollywood, and especially Warner Brothers, couldn't do without the cigarette prop. The loss of the Overseas Market and government action against "blind" theater bookings resulted in tighter budgets, iron-fisted production schedules and a concentration on cheap interiors that reeked of a rancid nocturnal America—murky light, rain-glistening streets, neon flickering "Hotel" and "Eats," smoke-blanketed bars and cocktail lounges, rain-splashed windshields, high-heels clicking, coffee-cup ashtrays, rooms of hideous knickknacks, and: Dan Duryea, Ella Raines, Veronica Lake, Bogart, Bacall, Stanwyck, Bette Davis, Joan Crawford, Alan Ladd, Lizabeth Scott, Wendell Corey, Laird Cregar, George Sanders, Joan Bennett, Zachary Scott, Eve Arden, Lana Turner, John Garfield, Martha Vickers, Elisha Cook, Jr., Ida Lupino, Robert Montgomery, Elsa Lanchester, George Macready, Peter Lorre, Sydney Greenstreet, Albert Basserman, Mary Beth Hughes, Lynn Bari, Evelyn Ankers, Veda Ann Borg, Belita, Audrey Totter, etc.

Bill Mauldin might have sold more cigarettes than Bogart and all of Hollywood. His *Stars and Stripes* cartoons of dogface noncoms "Willie and Joe" always slogging forward, bitching, bristle-bearded, with a lit or unlit "butt" protruding—were "the way it was" for the World War II foot soldier. Mauldin's graphic comments were drawn in mud, blood, wisecracks and prayer, and were an uncompromising negation of all the hymns of glory ever raised to war.

The Last Cigarette Generation came of smoking age during World War II, and if they smoked, they smoked *Lucky Strike, Chesterfield* or *Camel*. If eccentric, they might try *Spud, Home*

And so tomorrow morning will be one more Quits! Another—"just like that!" And if, as Scott Fitzgerald insisted, "there are no second acts in American lives," then in some not too distant time we will have again that "first delicious smoke." Meanwhile ... GobbleGobble GobbleGobbleGobbleGobbleGobbleGobbleGobbleGobbleGobbleGobb leGobbleGobbleGobbleGobbleGobbleGobbleGobbleGobbleGobble!!!!!

Run or *Picayune,* or experiment with one of the snob or foreign brands—*Murad, Melachrino, Players, Senior Service.* But for serious cigarette smoking there was *Lucky Strike, Chesterfield* or *Camel.*

The Fifties brought the kings, the filter kings, the mentholated: a battery of brands, millimeters, tables, tars and resins that read like a Manual of Small Arms Ammunition! "Cigarette fiefs" were created within the tobacco companies roughly analogous to General Motors. If Pontiac could compete with Buick, then within, say, *Philip Morris, Marlboro* (filter tip, 80 mm. and 85 mm.) and *Parliament* (filter tip, 80 mm. and 85 mm.) could compete with each other and with the parent *Philip Morris,* regular and long. The Last Cigarette Generation's smoking taste "boggled" at the choices—the tobacco manufacturers' "health-scare" sales efforts to combat a final, serious judgment on the "harms" of smoking. When Mayo Clinic head Dr. Charles W. Mayo feebly insisted: "I just don't believe smoking causes lung cancer," the game, the jig, the "smoke" was up!

The Last Cigarette Generation ended a long run—a full Centennial since that "discovery" in the Crimea and the births of those "good and bad boys of English Smoking" Sherlock Holmes and Oscar Wilde. Ian Fleming and his *James Bond* would persist into the Sixties, but smokes, like the Indians, were now "with reservations."

Some members of that Last Cigarette Generation, oblivious to all the smoke signals and true to their 70 mm. darlin's in their fashion, still remember and practice Tex Williams' country-and-western hit of the Forties—*Smoke! Smoke! Smoke! (That Cigarette)* ... tell St. Peter at the Golden Gate, that you hates to make him wait, but you gotta have another cigarette. . . !"

Still Smoking

I fled Him, down the nights and down the days;
I fled Him, down the arches of the years;
I fled Him, down the labyrinthine ways
Of my own mind; and in the midst of tears
I hid from Him, and under running laughter.
Up vistaed hopes I sped;
And shot, precipitated,
Adown Titanic glooms of the chasmèd fears,
From those strong Feet that followed, following after.

—Francis Thompson,
from THE HOUND OF HEAVEN, 1895

PHOTO CREDITS

Pp. 33-43, Ernest Trova Collection. P. 44, Culver Pictures, Inc. P. 45, Culver Pictures, Inc. P. 46, Harris Lewine Collection (4). P. 47, Harris Lewine Collection. P. 48, (clockwise) Harris Lewine Collection; Culver Pictures, Inc.; Harris Lewine Collection. P. 81, (clockwise) Culver Pictures, Inc.; Brown Bothers; Lou Bernstein. P. 82, (clockwise) Culver Pictures, Inc.; Harris Lewine Collection; Brown Brothers. P. 83, (clockwise) Culver Pictures, Inc.; Brown Brothers; Culver Pictures, Inc. P. 84, (clockwise) Culver Pictures, Inc. (2); Brown Brothers. P. 85, (clockwise) The Granger Collection; Mrs. John Held, Jr.; Culver Pictures, Inc. P. 86, Culver Pictures, Inc. (2). P. 87, (clockwise) Photo Files; Harris Lewine Collection (2); Culver Pictures, Inc. P. 88, Culver Pictures, Inc. P. 89, (clockwise) Culver Pictures, Inc.; Harris Lewine Collection; Photo Files (2). P. 90, (clockwise) Photo Files (2); Culver Pictures, Inc. (2). P. 91, Richard Merkin Collection; Photo Files; Culver Pictures, Inc.; Harris Lewine Collection; P. 92, (clockwise) Harris Lewine Collection; Brown Brothers; Harris Lewine Collection. P. 93, (clockwise) The Bettmann Archive; Richard Merkin Collection; Photo Files; Culver Pictures, Inc.; Harris Lewine Collection; P. 94, (clockwise) Harris Lewine Collection; Culver Pictures, Inc.; Photo Files; Culver Pictures, Inc. P. 95, (clockwise) Photo Files; Brown Brothers; Photo Files. P. 96, (clockwise) The Granger Collection; Harris Lewine Collection; The Granger Collection; Harris Lewine Collection. P. 97, (clockwise) Culver Pictures, Inc.; Barry Zaid; Harris Lewine Collection. P. 98, (clockwise) Photo Files (2); Harris Lewine Collection; Photo Files. P. 99, (clockwise) Photo Files (2); Culver Pictures, Inc. P. 100 (clockwise) Frank Driggs Collection; Photo Files (2); Harris Lewine Collection (2); P. 101, Gjon Mili from Ernest Smith Collection. P. 102, (clockwise) The Granger Collection; Culver Pictures, Inc. P. 103, (clockwise) The Granger Collection; Photo Files; The Granger Collection; Harris Lewine Collection. P. 104, (clockwise) Wide World Photos, Inc.; Brown Brothers; Horst Tappe. P. 105, (clockwise) Frank Driggs Collection; Les Zeiger Collection (7). P. 106, Harris Lewine Collection; The Bettmann Archive; Harris Lewine Collection. P. 107, (clockwise) Harris Lewine Collection; The Bettmann Archive; Harris Lewine Collection (2). P. 108, (clockwise) The Granger Collection (2); Frank Driggs Collection. P. 109, Harris Lewine Collection (3). P. 110, (clockwise) Culver Pictures, Inc.; Harris Lewine Collection. P. 111, (clockwise) Harris Lewine Collection (2); Karsh, Ottowa; Les Zeiger Collection. P. 112, (clockwise) The Nostalgia Shop; United Features Syndicate, Inc. P. 127, Harris Lewine Collection.

PRINTER:
The Chaucer Press, Inc.
Edward A. Simmons, President

PRODUCTION CONSULTANT:
Frank Franzo
The Chaucer Press, Inc.

COLOR SEPARATIONS:
Muller Color Plate

BINDER:
The Book Press, Inc.